Read the Face

Read the Face

Face Reading for Success
in Your Career, Relationships,
and Health

ERIC STANDOP

with Elisa Petrini

ST. MARTIN'S
ESSENTIALS
New York

First published in the United States by St. Martin's Essentials, an imprint of St. Martin's Publishing Group

READ THE FACE. Copyright © 2019 by Eric Standop. Illustrations copyright © 2019 by Yuliya Yarmolenka. All rights reserved. Printed in the United States of America. For information, address St. Martin's Publishing Group, 120 Broadway, New York, NY 10271.

The illustrations in this book were created by Yuliya Yarmolenka (yyarmolenka.com).

www.stmartins.com

The Library of Congress Cataloging-in-Publication Data is available upon request.

ISBN 978-1-250-21705-9 (hardcover)
ISBN 978-1-250-21706-6 (ebook)

Our books may be purchased in bulk for promotional, educational, or business use. Please contact your local bookseller or the Macmillan Corporate and Premium Sales Department at 1-800-221-7945, extension 5442, or by email at MacmillanSpecialMarkets@macmillan.com.

First Edition: October 2019

10 9 8 7 6 5 4 3 2 1

Contents

We see that the internal character of a man is often expressed in his exterior appearance, even in the manner of his walking and in the sound of his voice. Likewise the hidden character of things is to a certain extent expressed in their outward forms.

—Paracelsus

God has given you one face, and you make yourselves another.

—William Shakespeare

Nature gives you the face you have at twenty. Life shapes the face you have at thirty. But at fifty, you get the face you deserve.

—Coco Chanel

You have three faces. The first face, you show to the world.
The second face, you show to your close friends and your family.
The third face, you never show anyone.

—Japanese proverb

PART I

The Art and Science of Face Reading

1

Our First Language

I am a face reader. And so are you.

This skill is so critical to our survival that we have dedicated brain circuits for processing facial information. Imaging can pinpoint the exact place in the brain where our face-reading network lies. Scientists are still exploring how these neural circuits develop, but most believe that we're born face readers, at least to some extent. From the moment of birth—before its eyes can even focus—a baby is wired to seek out faces. Within hours, a baby can tell its mother's face from a female stranger's, and in just a few months it grows expert at identifying sex, race, emotions, and other basic traits.

This face-to-face connection is the child's first language. It is so potent that newborns are drawn even to facelike configurations, a row of two (or three or more) objects above a single one. But they do not respond to the same configuration—or even a human face—upside down.

I once had a funny experience at a corporate retreat, where I'd been invited to address some two hundred software engineers.

I had to laugh when the executive director warned that they'd introduce me as a "life coach," since "face reader" sounded too esoteric. But in fact I was planning to talk about life—about what our faces (and those of others) reveal about the way we live.

I began my speech by drawing a large oval on the whiteboard, with a short vertical line in the middle and a horizontal one below it. Then I stood back and invited comments.

Minutes passed, with everyone silent. I was getting nervous, but then, at last, a hand shot up.

"What do you see?" I asked.

"The OFF button on the remote control," the guy said.

What I had drawn, of course, was not an OFF button but the outline of a face, with the vertical line representing the nose and the horizontal one the mouth. But since my drawing didn't have eyes, no one could guess what it represented. That's how deeply we're imprinted with the two-objects-above-a-single-one model of the human countenance. Our instant interpretation of that image as a face is the reason that emojis—just a couple of dots and a line—can convey a world of meaning.

In time, when a newborn can distinguish features, it will literally see the love in its mother's eyes, her pupils enlarged with emotion. That's why teddy bears have black button eyes—they're all pupil—and probably why, as studies show, men are attracted to women with big pupils. Centuries ago, to be alluring, Italian women would dilate their pupils with the extract of a plant that got the name "beautiful lady," or belladonna.

This attraction to large pupils is primal and unconscious. As we grow up, we consciously gather data on others from multiple sources: their tone of voice, words, body language, hairstyles and clothing, and even the context in which we see them. We may be less aware of our face-reading powers, but the brain circuits producing them continue to fire, sparking gut feelings and intuitions.

In fact, research shows that fusiform gyrus, the specific area of the brain triggered by faces, continues to develop from infancy on.[1] Other complex visual-processing systems, like place recognition, are more static. As we mature, we grow to recognize the much wider range of faces necessary to navigate our broadening social networks. We also get increasingly better at distinguishing similar faces. By adulthood, we range from limited to gifted in our ability to identify faces, but on average, we remember and recognize some 20 percent of the people we've seen.

Roughly 2.5 percent of Americans fall at the low end of the identification spectrum because of "prosopagnosia," or face blindness, which may be inborn or acquired though trauma or diseases like Alzheimer's.[2] People with prosopagnosia have trouble distinguishing familiar faces, though they can readily identify other objects. The title character in the famous book by neurologist Oliver Sacks, *The Man Who Mistook His Wife for a Hat,* has a form of prosopagnosia. He identifies his wife by her voice and other people in his life, like his brother, by such specific features as big teeth. In middle age, Sacks himself, who'd never recognized his own reflection in a mirror, finally confronted his own face blindness.

The opposite of face blindness is "super-recognition," an extraordinary gift for identifying faces. The estimated 2 percent of people who are super-recognizers may memorize and recognize as many as 80 percent of the faces they see.[3] New Scotland Yard employs an elite super-recognizer squad to catch criminals by studying footage from London's million-plus surveillance cameras. Finding a needle in the haystack—a person filmed at a crime scene who has, say, a mug shot in the system—requires the uncanny ability to pick out a face on grainy, low-resolution video and match it with that of the known offender. Detective Chief Inspector Mick Neville, who created the unit, calls face recognition the "third revolution" of forensics, after fingerprints and DNA.

His squad has had surprising success. After civil unrest in 2011, computer face-recognition software could spot only one rioter from 200,000 hours of footage, while a single super-recognizer identified 190. According to published statistics, 73 percent of the squad's identifications have led to criminal charges. But what troubles rights advocates is that 13 percent, even after independent review by a second super-recognizer, have led to false arrests.[4]

An inevitable problem in facial analysis—whether human or electronic—is that it's only as accurate as its database. Humans, from birth onward, can best identify and read faces of the ethnicity we see most. White people tend to be better at recognizing white faces, black people at recognizing black faces, Asians at recognizing Asians, and so on.

Face-recognition technology, though vastly improved since 2011, shows the same bias. In a 2018 study of the capacity to read gender from a photo, three leading systems—those of Microsoft, IBM, and Megvii of China—detected faces of white or light-skinned men with an error rate of less than 1 percent. But when it came to spotting darker female faces, Microsoft's system had an error rate of 21 percent, while IBM's and Megvii's rates approached 35 percent.[5]

Also in 2018, the American Civil Liberties Union (ACLU) tested Amazon's system, used by some police departments, by running photos of all members of Congress against 25,000 published mug shots. No less than twenty-eight lawmakers were identified as criminals. Most were African American or Hispanic, including such well-known figures as congressmen John Lewis of Georgia and Bobby L. Rush of Illinois. The finding led the ACLU to condemn face-recognition technology as "flawed, biased, and dangerous."[6]

Even so, at this point face-recognition technology is largely unregulated. An estimated 117 million Americans, disproportionately nonwhite, appear in law enforcement databases.[7] The FBI has its own database of faces, which is reportedly smaller and less sophisticated than Facebook's cache of more than 2 billion images.[8] As government agencies and private companies—without restriction and oversight—amass data from millions of unsuspecting people's faces, the vast potential for abuse of the technology is obvious.

Fear of such abuse prompted two Stanford University scientists to test whether a facial-analysis program could guess people's sexual orientation. From public dating sites, they collected 35,000 photos of self-described gay and heterosexual people, all white, and had a widely used algorithm assess them for subtle differences. They then plugged in images of random faces and asked the computer to judge their sexual orientation. The results were chilling: the algorithm picked the correct sexual orientation 71 percent of the time for women and 81 percent of the time for men. When the computer was shown five images of a person, instead of one, the accuracy rose to 83 percent for women and 91 percent for men.[9]

Scientists at Shanghai Jiao Tong University applied the same method, using 1,856 images of men aged eighteen to fifty-five, to distinguish criminals from law-abiding citizens. Their algorithm detected the criminals among the randomly chosen faces with an accuracy of 89.5 percent and—especially relevant for our purposes—pinpointed the specific features that made them different. These traits included a curvature of the upper lip that was, on average, 23 percent greater than in the law-abiding group, a 6 percent shorter distance between the inner corners of the eyes, and an angle that was 20 percent narrower between two lines drawn from the tip of the nose to the corners of the mouth.[10]

The Chinese study was small and based on an algorithm created for Asian faces. Like the Stanford one, it raises frightening issues of invasion of privacy that are beyond the scope of this book. But because they have so many applications—airport security, law enforcement, medical diagnosis, and more—facial recognition and analysis are among the hottest fields in technology, growing faster than we can easily control or even imagine.

These new technologies have sparked a resurgence of interest in our human capacity for face reading. Dismissed in the West as a pseudoscience for most of the twentieth century, it is now studied at such prominent universities as the University of California at Berkeley, New York University, Stanford, and Princeton, to name a few. Some of these researchers still reject face reading as physiognomy, the practice of judging character from faces that dates back thousands of years, as we'll discuss in chapter 3, "Face Reading in History."

Critics of face reading attribute traits that humans, as opposed to machines, read into faces as stereotyping. But even the most skeptical acknowledge that we're hardwired to assess people instantly from their appearance. As scientist Alexander Todorov of Princeton, an authority on first impressions, writes, "Seeing a face for less than one-tenth of a second is sufficient to make up our minds. . . ."[11]

Over the past few decades, dozens of studies have demonstrated that, when shown the image of a face—whether human or computer generated—most subjects will define its personality the same way. To make their experiments uniform, psychologists usually have subjects rate personalities on what they call the "big five" traits: extraversion, agreeableness, conscientiousness, emotional stability/neuroticism, and openness to experience. Consensus on the personalities that faces express shows up even in research on children.

For example, in a pair of 2014 studies, scientists discovered that three- to four-year-olds could consistently distinguish between faces that were "nice" and "mean," "strong" and "not very strong," and "smart" and "not very smart." Averaging the responses across categories, 72 percent of the three- to four-year-olds agreed on the traits the faces revealed. Among five- and six-year-olds, the degree of agreement was higher (81 percent); and among seven- to ten-year-olds, it rose to 88 percent. Among adults, the degree of agreement was nearly the same as among the seven- to ten-year-olds (89 percent).[12]

Still, many scientists argue that personality can't be gleaned from the face alone. For one thing, they say, faces change from moment to moment, as we'll discuss in chapter 7, "The World of Expression." For another, they warn of "overgeneralization," or making too much of detectable cues. One confusing cue they cite is attractiveness, which can have a halo effect, making the person seem lovable, kind, and so on simply because of being beautiful. While we are all drawn to attractive people (see "The Perfect Face," which lists traits that research shows make people attractive), in face reading the concept of beauty is not especially relevant.

Instead, what we look for is an overall picture. We know from research on face blindness that the human brain and a computer algorithm process faces differently. Rather than break out features, the brain considers the face holistically, as one image. That's a major reason why this book is not a how-to guide, offering lists of facial characteristics with assigned meanings.

A computer might have a database of images of, say, a thousand

The Perfect Face

Is there such a thing as the perfect face? Many studies have been done on what makes faces attractive. University of Toronto psychologists Daniel E. Re and Nicholas O. Rule, surveying the research, high-lighted certain aspects that appeal across cultures, as well as probable reasons:

- Even skin tone and texture, likely because they suggest youth and health. Study subjects shown a face with color variations smoothed out judged the person to be five years younger, and one with wrinkles smoothed out to be as much as fifteen years younger.

- Skin color, with red tones (but not too much red) suggesting well-oxygenated blood and cardiovascular fitness and yellow tones (in Causcasians, Asians, and Africans) implying good immune function. Yellow skin tones come from carotenoid compounds in fruits and vegetables, which are depleted by illness. One 2012 study found that eating three to four servings of fruits and vegetables per day for six weeks increased carotenoids enough to make people look more attractive.

- Averageness, an observation first made in 1878 (and more recently tested using computer-generated composites), possibly because faces deviating wildly from the norm might indicate poor health. But attractiveness is not necessarily the same as beauty. The most attractive faces have some special eye-catching feature.

- Symmetry, but not two sides of the face that are mirror-images, which would look weird and unnatural. People across cultures prefer faces with their basic structures aligned, if not perfectly, though the link to underlying health is not as certain.

- Fleshiness (adiposity) of the face reflects a person's BMI or Body

Mass Index. People tend to prefer faces reflecting a BMI of approximately 20, which is right in the middle of the normal range, to faces that look underweight or overweight.

• Femininity and masculinity have been much studied as factors in attractiveness, with uncertain results. Scientists believe that the hormone estrogen, governing the development of women's faces, gives them the features usually defined as feminine: large eyes, full lips, a small and pointed chin, and high cheekbones. More feminine features imply higher levels of estrogen, suggesting fertility, the theory holds. Subjects of studies, when asked to make a neutral face more attractive, usually enhance the femininity of its features.

Masculine features, established by testosterone, include a prominent brow ridge, high cheekbones, and a square jaw. But men's faces—unlike women's, in which femininity is correlated with attractiveness—are not necessarily most appealing when they appear most masculine. Some studies show that women prefer more feminized features in both Asian and Caucasian men, others have shown no preference, and still others have shown that women's preferences may vary by context. Researchers speculate that a masculine appearance, signaling high testosterone, may be linked to undesirable personality traits, including aggressive behavior, infidelity, and lack of interest in parenting. Attraction to masculine looks was highest in areas where the standard of living was lowest. There may be other, as yet undetermined, factors that lend allure to a male face.[13]

For a face reader, the perfect face, male or female, is one that conveys authenticity. In chapter 12, "Perception," I'll describe my own vision of the perfect face: the "enlightened" visage.

criminals' faces and sift through them to see what they have in common. But humans confront each new face in real time, taking in its fixed features, like the eyes, nose, and mouth; watch it shift through a range of microexpressions; and draw a conclusion, usually unconsciously, through intuition.

All this new scientific interest is simply, if powerfully, validating what human beings have known for thousands of years. As psychology professors Ran Hassin and Yaacov Trope write, in an account of their studies of faces published in the *Journal of Personality and Social Psychology,* "It seems only reasonable to assume that if the mind devotes special brain resources to processing faces, it will try to extract as much information from the face as it can."[14]

I've spent my adult life, as I'll discuss in chapter 2, studying the ancient systems that have tried to "extract information" by making our innate, automatic assessments of faces more conscious. Every face is a complex map of life, with inborn traits, characteristics developed through experience, talents, reflections of health, signs of shifting emotional weather, and more. By telling the stories I've observed in faces and explaining my interpretations, I hope to help you recognize your own intuitive powers and begin, more consciously, to develop them.

By awakening your instinctive capacity to read faces, you can achieve a deeper understanding of others—and, even more, yourself.

2

Eric Is an Egg

I stumbled on face reading in the effort to heal myself.

I grew up in Karlsruhe, Germany, founded in 1715—a city that's young by European standards. The seat of Germany's highest courts, it's also home to nine universities. Maybe that's why it has produced so many innovators, like Karl Drais, inventor of the two-wheel bicycle; Karl Benz, who built the first car; the father of electromagnetism, Heinrich Rudolph Hertz; and the pioneering psychoanalyst Erik Erikson.

Nothing in my youth suggested I'd become a face reader. Quite the opposite: I was analytic, business-minded, and so driven that I've jokingly been called a Jack Russell, an eager, energetic terrier. After graduating from the university with a degree in teaching and communications, I worked as a radio announcer and journalist, as well as behind the scenes in television production and promotions. By my early thirties, I was the regional second in command of UFA Cinema, overseeing the theme parks and more than a thousand employees of one of Europe's top theater chains.

Then I crashed. Strangely, my collapse was heralded by a movie.

In *The Devil's Advocate,* Keanu Reeves plays a lawyer working at a cutthroat firm. His blind ambition costs him his wife, who's raped and commits suicide, and yokes him to his boss, Al Pacino, who turns out to be Satan. When Reeves blames him for her death, among other evil machinations, Satan protests that Reeves willingly forfeited his life for success—that he could have quit anytime. At the end, Reeves tries to take a moral stand but, corrupted by vanity, ultimately can't.

The film shocked me to the bone. I so strongly identified with the Keanu Reeves character that I couldn't get him out of my mind. Constantly traveling to troubleshoot problems, I, too, sacrificed everything for work—all my energy, my relationships, my humanity. My already poor sleep progressed to full-blown insomnia. I broke out in weird, intensely itchy rashes, among other hard-to-treat ailments. The conclusion was inescapable that, unlike Reeves, I had to swallow my professional pride and quit. I was in burnout.

At age thirty-four, I scaled back to a job with more regular hours as public relations director for a computer games company. In a few months I felt as cramped as a horse in a cage: trapped, bored, and yearning to run. The CEO spotted my restlessness and urged me to do more. So, overnight, my duties expanded to encompass marketing, web services, and event planning. I was so successful that I was soon tapped for an even more challenging, high-stress role coordinating marketing activities worldwide.

Again, I hit the road, managing offices in tech hubs including Paris, London, and San Francisco. And, again, my skin was on fire with new diseases. I was choking for breath from asthma, possibly triggered by a new spate of allergies that left me unable to eat anything but potatoes, brown rice, and a few vegetables. Even those foods gave me constant diarrhea, stripping pounds from my skeletal frame. I developed a stomach ulcer. My left shoulder froze, crippling my arm. I kept traveling, ignoring the signs.

Then one day, I couldn't get out of bed. My legs simply failed to respond to my brain's commands. Terrified, I managed to roll to the floor and eventually recovered enough mobility to start making the rounds of doctors. I collected a laundry list of diagnoses—fifteen different conditions—and referrals, including one to a urologist. He was a heavyset man with the gray skin and stained fingers of a smoker. "My exam didn't reveal anything special," he said. "Just the normal changes of age. But I can tell you one thing: Whatever's wrong with you, it's grave. You look like death."

Was he crazy? How could a man with such obvious bad habits dare to call me mortally ill? But no one could pinpoint a cause other than stress, and I was too debilitated to work. So I quit my job and, over months of backpacking around the world, regained a small measure of health.

On a beach in South Africa, I met my first face reader. I was trying to kite surf and, being a Jack Russell, was bursting with frustration. An acquaintance tried to distract me, saying, "You know, there's a nice bar around the corner. An old man there reads faces, and he can tell everything about you."

"Come on," I said. "That's a load of bull." But we made a bet. He'd pay for my weekend if the old man was wrong, and I'd cover his if the reading proved true.

In the bar, the old man, toothless and dressed like a bum, sat in a corner walled in by empty beer bottles. "What do you see in my face?" I demanded, slamming a lager on the table.

He was unfazed. Scrutinizing me with a clinical stare, he

ticked off some obvious traits: aggressiveness, impatience, being driven to lead but lacking the ability, and so on. When I acted skeptical, he turned to my health. That's when he blew me away. Not only did he identify my fifteen diagnosed ailments, he read the past, mentioning a couple of hernia repairs and my childhood lung infections. He judged my current problems to be the result of inflammation in my intestine.

What a powerful gift, I thought. If I could apply it in business, I'd be a genius. Later I learned that face reading is commonly used in Asia to size up the competition in negotiations. Every culture in the world has a face-reading tradition, though in the West, in the realm of health, it's been largely supplanted by technology and is otherwise something of a lost art.

Back in Germany, I tried to learn more about face reading. All I could find was a kind of fortune-telling, using vaguely Chinese principles. Hoping to improve my health, I enrolled in nutrition courses but quickly got fed up. The instructor noticed that I was bored. "This field's too limited for you," she said. "And by the way, go easy on the coffee. It can upset your inflamed gut."

"How can you tell?" I asked.

"I can see it in your face." It turned out that she knew a real face reader, who lived near the Danish border, far to the north.

When I called, he urged me to visit the following week, to attend a "convention." That thrilled me—the chance to meet what I imagined would be the nation's top practitioners, gathered in one place. After driving for six hours, I pulled up at the tiny town hall, to find it ringed with booths advertising arcana involving angels, crystals, unicorns, and more, manned by people in flowing garments with long gray hair. I was shocked. With an hour to kill until my appointment, I locked myself in the car, trying to ignore the yoga class in the parking lot.

Finally, I met the reader, a serious-looking man of sixty something, I guessed, who, to my relief, was dressed normally. Suppressing my horror at the spiritualistic setting—repugnant to such a super-rational executive as myself—I told him about my life, my problems, and my experience in South Africa. "Thank you for your story," he said graciously. "Have a good trip back."

"What about my face?" I was outraged. "I drove hundreds of miles! Don't I even get a reading?"

"You already had a reading in South Africa," he told me. "I have nothing more to say."

The entire drive back, I was railing on the phone to friends about the "rip-off convention," the "charlatan" reader—on and on. But to my surprise, I got an e-mail from him a few weeks later, asking me to meet him three days hence in another small, faraway town. What nerve! My best friend, Bernd, encouraged me to go, since I knew people in a nearby city. The trip could be a little vacation if the reader's invitation turned out to be some gimmick.

The reader was staying in a bed-and-breakfast, where I found seven other people waiting. He came outside to address us. "Thank you all for coming," he said. "I don't have long to live, so I want to share my knowledge, if you're willing to learn. I've chosen you to be my last students."

He was not in his sixties, as I'd thought, but in his mideighties. "What's this going to cost?" I asked, smelling a scam.

"Nothing material," he said. "But, Eric, it will cost you your belief system."

He became my first master. Over the next year and a half, I followed him to schools, hospitals, and even a prison, where he did consultations, and sometimes just to train stations, where we'd practice facial analysis. From him I learned two European systems of face reading, both derived from ancient Greece. One was in the Hippocratic tradition, relating to health, and the other, springing from Aristotle's practice of physiognomy, focused more on personality. The study did upend my belief system, deepening and broadening my insight into my fellow human beings.

At the age of thirty-nine, I graduated from that first apprenticeship and founded a counseling business called Restart Life. Afraid that calling myself a face reader would be off-putting, I offered nutritional advice and personal training, based on the needs I saw in people's faces. The business, unfortunately, was too esoteric for the German public and failed miserably. I was not only hurt financially but also, because I was and remain a logical, science-minded person, pained at being perceived as some kind of novelty act, spiritualist, or freak. I badly wanted to pull the plug and go back to the business world, but my master urged me, "Keep going."

Needing a break and new inspiration, I headed to South America to see Machu Picchu and other ancient wonders. On one of my last days there, in Cartagena, Colombia, I overheard a guy talking to a bunch of American tourists. "That's the mouth of a passionate kisser," he was saying, and, "No one with those lips is a good lover." When the group dispersed, I approached and learned that he too was a face reader, one who focused mainly on love. There was an entire South American tradition of face reading grounded in principles different from those that I had learned. So I asked him to train me in what he knew. My classrooms this time were not hospitals and police stations but bars and other evening hangouts. Every night we went out to study couple's interactions or, interestingly, the expressions that made people attract or repel potential partners.

After those sessions, I was hooked. Face reading was an undeniably powerful tool, capable of revealing the full complexity of a human being, body and soul. Though I'd lost heart before my trip, I was now determined to dedicate my life to learning all I could about this profound discipline. To do so, I'd have to go to Asia, where face reading is a time-honored tool of the ancient system of healing called Traditional Chinese Medicine (TCM).

It's not like there was a school where I could enroll. Over the past five decades, as the West has embraced alternative medicine, institutes have sprung up around the world teaching acupuncture, herbalism, and other Eastern modes of treatment and diagnosis. But for Asian face reading, which until now has been little known in the West, there was only the old-fashioned path to knowledge. I'd have to find a Chinese master who would accept me as an apprentice.

I had an English friend living in Hong Kong, so I started there. At the famous Temple Street night market, face readers worked the crowds. I made the rounds, only to find that most offered tourists the same value as the hawkers of "authentic" antiques and jade. No one took me seriously except my friend, whose wife-to-be asked me to help her boss, who suffered from migraines.

The boss's face showed that, besides headaches, she had muscle cramps, mood swings, and a craving for sweets. These and other signs pointed to a deficiency of magnesium, the mineral supporting hundreds of chemical reactions in the body, some of which steady blood sugar and generate cell energy, as well as promote nerve and muscle function. On my advice, she took supplements and, just three days later, called to report a miracle. "These problems have plagued me for years," she said. "I can't believe it, but now they're gone!"

She ran the spa at an exclusive hotel and offered me a practitioner's job. As word spread, I was swamped with clients. Most of them were Asian, to my surprise—willing to take a chance on a European face reader. Then one day I picked up the phone to hear an angry voice demanding, "What are you doing in our city?"

"What do you mean?" I asked.

"You're no face reader," said the voice. "White men cannot read faces."

I agreed to meet the caller, who turned out to be a Chinese master in his eighties—almost a stereotype of the kind of teacher I'd sought. But he kept badgering about my race. I fought back, pointing out that he drank beer: "That's a German, not a Chinese thing," adding, "and how many Chinese people do yoga, which is Indian?"

He laughed at that, but we kept arguing back and forth. I didn't even notice that he revealed nothing of himself as he probed my character and grilled me about my training. A couple of hours passed, then, without warning, he proclaimed, "You will be my student!"

Still stung by his insults, I declined. "You want it," he insisted. Finally, his niece convinced me, explaining that he'd accepted very few students in his life. Only rarely, she said, would a master even consider a trainee who was Asian but not Chinese—who was, say, Japanese or Korean. It was thus inconceivable—and a tremendous honor—that he would choose a white apprentice like me.

So for the next six years, with breaks so I could work or visit home, I was his shadow. Training with a Chinese master is more oppressive than the military. I'd done my mandatory service in the parachute corps and hated every second—being told when to sleep, what to wear, and what to do. Now, I had all those constraints, plus a tougher one—being forbidden to question. I wasn't even allowed to comment on his readings or on his commands to perform tasks like cleaning his shoes. That kind of discipline was almost impossible for an executive, especially a quick and impatient one like me, used to issuing, not obeying, orders. But somehow I managed.

When he finally determined that I was ready, he inducted me into his circle of *sifus,* accomplished Chinese master readers. There was a lot of pushback—*He's too young. He's too modern and has even explained our art to groups, not just individual students*; and, of course, *He's white!* But, finally, a majority gave in. I was pronounced a *sifu.* My master was so proud. "Eric is white on the outside but yellow on the inside," he loved to say. "Eric is an egg."

3

Face Reading in History

It's not surprising that every culture has a face-reading tradition. Face readers are depicted in Egyptian hieroglyphics and in South American carvings. In India, the face-reading styles relate to Hindu religious beliefs. There may be twenty or more existing types in Africa. Lectura del Rostro, the method I learned in Colombia, probably has versions throughout Latin America. Chinese face reading is very well established, and other Asian countries, including Japan, have their own schools.

We trace European face reading back to the golden age of Greece, around the fifth century BC. The ancient Greek philosophers believed in physiognomy, the notion that the face reflects the personality. There's a famous story about Zopyrus, an early physiognomist, visiting Plato's academy in Athens, where philosophers gathered. There he met Plato's teacher, Socrates. Studying his face, he pronounced Socrates to be a skirt chaser, as well as dull and witless. The other members of Plato's circle laughed, but Socrates concurred with his reading. He was dissolute, slow, and stupid by nature, he confessed, and had to learn, through discipline and reason, to master these defects.

Plato's younger contemporary, Aristotle (384–322 BC), was one of the foremost intellectual figures in Western history. He significantly advanced every branch of knowledge of his time, including the sciences, from botany to zoology; all the arts; and all studies of the mind, including psychology and, of course, philosophy. The earliest surviving work on face reading, *Physiognomonics,* is attributed to him, though it was probably created by one of his disciples.

The work incorporated ideas from Aristotle's *History of Animals,* in which he connected physical features and personality traits. For example, he linked high foreheads to lethargy and wide ones to being high strung. Straight eyebrows signify a "soft" nature, while those angled toward the nose warn of a hot temper. Ears that stick out mark a person as a foolish chatterbox. Aristotle's insights often embraced the concept of the "mean," whether or not the middle ground was the most effectual—for example, he believed that the most deep-set eyes are the sharpest but that neutral ones (neither deep-set nor protruding) indicate the best character. Through the conquests of his student Alexander the Great, Aristotle's brand of physiognomy spread throughout the Middle East and as far afield as India.

In the same period, Hippocrates (460–375 BC), the father of modern medicine, incorporated face reading into his diagnostic methods. He is credited with identifying the combination of signs that herald impending death, including sharpening of the nose, sinking of the eyes, hollowing of the temples, coldness and curling of the ears, pallor, and hardening of the skin. This array of symptoms, called the Hippocratic face, is still considered, 2,500 years later, to be a valid index of failing health.

The ideas of Hippocrates are preserved in the Hippocratic corpus, a body of some seventy works, many of which were likely written by his disciples. The most famous treatises include *The Hippocratic Oath*, which today is still administered to would-be doctors; *Prognosticon*, thoughts on the likely progression and outcome of illnesses; and *Aphorisms*, a collection of observations (such as, "In whatever part of the body heat or cold is seated, there is disease") used as a medical school text for centuries. Hippocrates so revolutionized medicine that for a time after his death, advances in medicine slowed to a crawl because his ideas were too revered to question.

The role of face reading in medicine from Hippocrates on is evidenced by the many disorders with names featuring the Latin word *facies* ("face"), such as leonine facies (a form of leprosy), Cushingoid facies (Cushing's disease), snarling facies (myasthenia gravis), mouse facies (chronic kidney failure), and masklike facies (Parkinson's disease), among others.

In Europe, face reading was taught in major universities until the Middle Ages, when it detoured into fortune-telling and fell from favor. The Renaissance genius Leonardo da Vinci (1452–1519) dismissed it as "without scientific foundation" yet believed that facial lines offered clues to personality. For example, deep creases between the eyebrows, in his view, signified testiness.

Face reading had a major revival from the seventeenth through nineteenth centuries, with an infusion of new theories by such luminaries as the polymath physician Sir Thomas Browne (1605–82), who wrote that faces bear "the motto of our souls" and who supposedly introduced the word *caricature,* meaning exaggeration of features to comment on character, into the English language. His work has been cited by writers ranging from Herman Melville and Edgar Allan Poe to Jorge Luis Borges and William Styron. Giambattista della Porta (1535–1615) used woodcuts of animals to illustrate human characteristics and to demonstrate that it was temperament, not the magic of the stars, that determined facial expressions. His important works involving face reading include *Magia Naturalis* and *De Humana Physiognomia*. In the eighteenth century, the Swiss theologian Johann Kaspar Lavater (1741–1801) built on the ideas of Browne, della Porta, and others to become a celebrated author and probably physiognomy's greatest popularizer.

Lavater's major four-volume work, *Physiognomische Fragmente,* published in German, was an encyclopedia of physiognomy created with the help of some of the great thinkers of his time, including Goethe. Its chief theory holds that, consciously or unconsciously, we assess personality and predict behavior by observing a person's face. Lavater believed that the fixed features of the face, such as the eyes, nose, and mouth, reveal the true moral nature of the person, while changing facial expressions can be more deceptive. The heavily illustrated work depicted formations of different features; discussed their interrelation (claiming, for example, that people with curved foreheads rarely have hooked noses); and offered general guidelines for interpretation, such as the idea that all shapes in the face made of straight lines convey strength, inflexibility, and intelligence, while all those made of curved lines suggest weakness, flexibility, and sensuality.

Lavater famously came up with one hundred rules for analyzing features, including his own. By those rules, his unexceptional nose was the kind associated with people "in some degree superior but never with such as are truly great and excellent."

Lavater's descriptive physiognomy was influential throughout Europe. Others steered physiognomy in a more anatomical direction. Dutch physiologist Petrus Camper (1722–89), a pioneer of comparative anatomy and anthropology, came up with a theory based on facial slope ("prognathism"). He compared the slope from nose to forehead of the skulls of apes and "modern" Africans and Europeans to the faces of ancient Greco-Roman statues. For the apes, the angle of the slope was 42 to 58 degrees; for Africans, it was 70 degrees; for Europeans, 80 degrees; and for the statues, representing the classical ideal of beauty, it was 95 to 100 degrees. Thus, Africans were the farthest removed from and Europeans closest to being perfect human specimens. This theory became a pillar of "scientific racism" or "race biology," the belief in physiological measurements supposedly "proving" the inferiority of certain races, that persisted into the twentieth century.

Scottish surgeon and gifted illustrator Sir Charles Bell (1774–1842), in *Essays on the Anatomy and Philosophy of Expression,* connected structures and muscles of the face to expressions of emotion, which he believed emerged from the intellect. These facial expressions, in his view, were unique to the individual, set humans apart from animals, and demonstrated mankind's special relationship with the Creator.

Guillaume-Benjamin-Amand Duchenne de Boulogne (1806–75), a neurology innovator, confirmed Bell's idea by stimulating facial muscles with a novel tool, electricity, to form expressions. He documented his experiments using another new technology, photography, and published the astonishing images in a book, *The Mechanism of Human Physiognomy.* Unlike his predecessors, he rejected the notion that facial features reflected moral fiber and believed that expressions were a "gateway to the soul"—to current mental states. This study of emotions and passions, as opposed to fixed personality traits, is called pathognomy. Duchenne believed that, by drawing on dedicated muscle groups, our faces can express at least sixty different emotions, which all humans convey the same way—that facial expressions are, in effect, a universal language.

One of those sixty expressions is the "Duchenne smile," which involves the contraction of two muscles, the zygomatic major (raising the corners of the mouth) and the orbicularis oculi (raising the cheeks and producing crow's-feet around the eyes). The double contraction is the sign of a genuine smile, which scientists now know is produced by a different area of the brain (the limbic system) than a phony "say-cheese" smile, which is controlled by the motor cortex.

Charles Darwin (1809-82), the eminent English naturalist, also believed that there are universal expressions of emotions, some of which—like eyebrows lifted in surprise—humans share with animals. This was a radical departure from Charles Bell's idea that facial expressions signified the special connection between man and God.

In 1872, Darwin published his third major work of evolutionary theory, this time covering the biological aspects of emotion, *The Expression of the Emotions in Man and Animals*. To develop it, he circulated a worldwide questionnaire on displays of emotion in different cultures, drew on his own anthropological notes from his travels and his observations of animals, conducted psychological experiments on his family and friends, and consulted with Duchenne and James Crichton-Browne, a British psychiatrist and neuroscientist. Darwin concluded that the facial muscles don't specialize to produce sixty different expressions of emotion, as Duchenne believed, but that muscles work together to produce a core group of expressions common to every culture: anger, fear, surprise, disgust, happiness, and sadness.

One of Darwin's great champions was Italian neurologist, anthropologist, and novelist Paolo Mantegazza (1831–1910), who is perhaps best known today for his enthusiastic experiments on the effects of cocaine on the human psyche (he was a fan). Greatly influenced by Darwin's work on expressions and Duchenne's photo studies, he documented expressions of pain inflicted by different sensory stimuli, such as a grimace from a bad smell and a frown from painful memories. Among other books on passions such as hate and love, Mantegazza published a major work, *Physiognomy and Expression,* that purported to be an "alphabet" of facial expressions of emotion, taking into account the proportions of the face. He classified facial expressions as emerging from the senses, the passions, and the intellect and also factored culture, gender, and historical period into his interpretations of their meaning.

An outlier among the neurologists and physiologists was the portrait painter Carl Huter (1861–1912), whose theory of psychophysiognomy sought "knowledge of human nature through body, life, soul, and facial expressions." He believed that psychophysiognomy was the fundamental science because we are capable of perceiving only the exterior of things and must rely on what we see to guess at the hidden interior. His observations of people's faces, heads, and body shapes, as well as facial expressions and gestures, led him to develop five categories of human nature—harmonious, disharmonious, nutritional, movement, and sensational—which he thought might be also replicated in the plant and animal realms. He struggled all his life to reconcile his theory with new discoveries in biology, physics, and anatomy, as well as astrology, psychology, and theology. Even today there are Huterite groups in Europe that continue his work on psychophysiognomy. Among the contemporary theorists originally inspired by Huter is respected naturopath Natale Ferronato, whose discipline, patho-physiognomics, seeks evidence of disease in the face.

Along with these philosophical, physiological, and psychological considerations of the face, there were pragmatic applications of physiognomy. In the mid-nineteenth century, Cesare Lombroso used physiognomy to launch the new science of criminology. Combining its classical principles with the fresh theories of Charles Darwin, Lombroso argued that criminals were "savage throwbacks" to a prior stage of human evolution. As such, the "born criminal" had "primitive" features like a low, sloping forehead; a large, forward-thrusting jaw; and a flattened or upturned nose. Left-handedness was another sign of villainy. These ideas might seem easy to debunk, since criminals don't look alike, but since they were so aligned with the biases of the time, they proved highly influential.

By the early twentieth century, physiognomy lost ground to new diagnostic technologies in medicine and new behavioral theories, from phrenology (the study of skull shapes) to psychoanalysis. Still, it has long been reflected in the idioms of every language: *in the twinkling of an eye, didn't bat an eye, raised an eyebrow, furrowed his brow, wrinkled her nose, paid through the nose,* and was *down in the mouth* are just a few examples in English.

While face reading has waxed and waned in the West, in Asia it has remained a respected discipline for thousands of years. Its cultural importance, especially in China, is affirmed by the fact that a map of ancient and modern face-reading principles appears on large Hong Kong banknotes. China had thriving schools of face reading as far back as 480 BC, and today certain masters from ancient times are still celebrated. The name of the discipline, Mien Shiang, literally means "face" (*mien*) "reading" (*shiang*).

The earliest Chinese face readers were probably followers of Lao-tzu, a supposed contemporary of Confucius (551–478 BC) and author of the *Tao Te Ching,* a guide for living simply, in harmony with a natural force known as the Tao, that is the foundational text of Taoism. Whether Lao-tzu actually existed is debatable. The name means "old master," and modern scholars believe he may have been an amalgam of sages and his book a collection of their teachings. A central figure in Chinese culture, he's revered both as a teacher and a deity.

The first known face reader may have been Guigi Xiansheng, a hermit known as the Sage of Ghost Valley, who was the putative author of the *Guiguzi,* a book of Taoist ideas on politics and the theory of opposites, *yin* and *yang.* Tradition holds that he was the teacher of Sun Bin (died 316 BC), famous for expanding the ancient treatise *The Art of War* by Sun Tzu, and Pang Juan (died 342 BC). The two were close friends who became heads of warring states and mortal enemies, and to this day they are commemorated as door gods in Chinese temples.

In 221 BC, Qin Shi Huang (259–210 BC) conquered the fractious Chinese states and became the first emperor of a united country. His achievements include construction of the initial Great Wall protecting China from Eurasian marauders. To erase the past, he ordered book burnings (retaining copies for the royal libraries) and restricted certain traditional practices to his palace, including face reading.

He used face readers to help with the construction of his tomb, which is one of the world's marvels. Larger than any existing city of its time, it had a burial chamber with the constellations painted on its ceiling, according to historical accounts, and below it a representation of the land, with one hundred streams of mercury, which flowed mechanically, representing rivers. Protecting the tomb was a huge pit, about three-quarters of a mile square, filled with a vast army of life-size terra-cotta soldiers.

Legend holds that, to create the soldiers, face readers were sent to scour the countryside for model faces bearing signs of bravery, strength, and loyalty. Some speculate that molds were created for ten or more different types of faces, which were then painted to give each of them individual features. Every one of the roughly eight thousand statues—armored warriors, spear-carrying chari-oteers, cavalrymen in pillbox hats, kneeling archers, commanders, and more—has a different visage.

In the third century AD, China split again into what's called the Three Kingdoms, one of which, Shu Han, was headed by former warlord Lui Bei. His most trusted aide, Zhuge Liang (181–234), was a military strategist, eventual ruler of a province, inventor, and author of the Chinese classic works *Thirty-Six Strat-agems* and *Mastering the Art of War*. He is credited with being a mas-ter diplomat, who supposedly released a captured rebel seven times to ensure his complete surrender. He was also an accomplished face reader, charged with choosing those best suited to fill important po-sitions, and wrote books on his techniques. Venerated in China as a semideity, with temples built in his honor, he is a prominent char-acter in the fourteenth-century Chinese novel by Luo Guanzhong, *Romance of the Three Kingdoms,* which is known today through various films, TV series, manga comics, and video games.

A few centuries later, Yang Chiu Pu (581–688) won renown for combining face reading with the ancient art of feng shui, or balancing the energies of people in spaces. Broken down, his name means "willow tree" (Yang) and "for the poor" (Chui Pu), so he was clearly a respected protector and mentor.

His contemporary Li Shen Feng (589–686), at just thirteen years old, was summoned to read the faces of the family of the warlord-governor of the Shanxi Province, Li Yuan (566–635). Li Shen Feng singled out the warlord's second son, Li Shimin (598–649), as combining the qualities of a dragon and a phoenix, predicting that he would rise to power in twenty years.

After subduing various rivals, in 618 Li Yuan launched the Tang Dynasty, ruling under the name of Emperor Gaozu. Though he reformed the legal system and reunited the country, his reign lasted only eight years. In 626, Li Shimin killed his brothers and forced his father's abdication, right on schedule with Li Shen Feng's prediction.

Li Shimin, ruling as Emperor Taizong, became one of China's greatest leaders. Lin Shen Feng became his close adviser. One day, he happened to spot a young girl, Wu Zetian, among the emperor's hundred concubines and proclaimed, improbably, that she would be the future empress of China.

Wu Zetian (624–705) was one of the few girls of the time to be educated before she was made an imperial concubine at age fourteen. Never one of Taizong's favorites, she was given secretarial duties and so continued her studies. She also took up with Li Zhi, the youngest of the emperor's fourteen sons. After Taizong's death, she was banished to a convent, along with his other childless concubines, until Li Zhi rescued her. When he took the throne as Emperor Gaozong, Wu Zetian became his chief concubine, then empress consort and regent. Through years of bloody intrigues, she steadily gained power. Once Gaozong died, she proclaimed herself empress and ruled from 690 to 705—just as Li Shen Feng had foretold—as the only female sovereign in Chinese history.

These are just some of the legendary Chinese face readers, and over the centuries many more would emerge. In the modern era, Chiang Kai-shek (1887–1975), president of the Republic of China from 1928 until his death (ruling on the mainland until 1949, when he was deposed by Mao Tse-tung, and from 1950 on in Taiwan) relied on the guidance of face readers.

Face reading continued to flourish in Taiwan and Hong Kong after 1966, when Mao Tse-tung's Cultural Revolution began. Though Mao (1893–1976), consulted face readers, the practice itself, along with such traditions as feng shui, tai chi, and qi gong, was lumped into the Four Olds (old ideas, old customs, old culture, and old habits of mind) that were banned, with harsh enforcement, for the decade the Cultural Revolution lasted.

Two generations after Mao's death, Chinese face reading is being revived, though some of the ancient lore and wisdom has been lost. There's also some confusion about its place in the culture. Some whose parents and grandparents were forbidden to use it think of it is as entertainment, like fortune-telling, rather than as a potent method of analysis. However, it's considered an invaluable tool in Traditional Chinese Medicine. It's also welcomed in the business world—in Asia, the Middle East, and beyond—by corporate leaders seeking an edge.

Because Chinese face reading has such a strong, codified history, its principles underlie most professional face reading today, including my own. In chapter 4, "The Art of Face Reading," I'll explain the most commonly used approaches.

4

The Art of Face Reading

Over several millennia, naturally, many different schools of Chinese face reading, or Mien Shiang, developed. In my readings, I draw on different ones from time to time, as well as on the European and South American training I describe in chapter 2, "Eric Is an Egg." In addition, as you'll find in part II, "The Face in Stories," I occasionally refer to certain esoteric Chinese maps of the face, such as a destiny chart that links 108 different points on the face linked to the years of a person's life, for extra insight.

I also incorporate the ideas of the influential psychologist Paul Ekman, among others, on microexpressions, which are instant emotional reactions, some voluntary and some involuntary. Microexpressions are universal, meaning that the same ones are observed in every culture and, studies show, even in blind people who could not have picked them up through observation. Finally, like anyone who studies people, I remain alert to body language and other physical personality cues. Every source of information is worth considering. Chapter 7, "The World of Expression," explains microexpressions and other tools of perception.

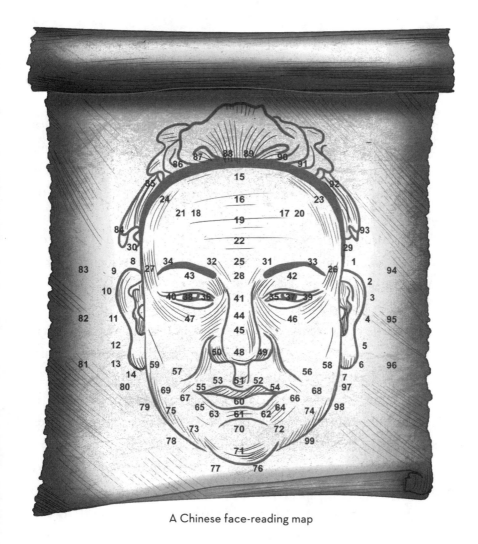

A Chinese face-reading map

These multiple influences define my face-reading style and philosophy, along with a few essential principles:

1. Face reading is not psychotherapy or fortune-telling. It is observation of the face at a certain moment in time. Sometimes I see clues to the past that are worth exploring because they affect the present, but digging into history to resolve problems is not my goal. Similarly, I might see possible outcomes of the way a client is living and discuss the choices or challenges that might lie ahead.

But that's not the same as predicting the future, which is more of a magic act.

2. Concepts like "good" and "bad" and "positive" and "negative" have no place in my professional philosophy. Each of us is born with traits, burnished by our life experience, that we can use to our benefit or detriment. I call this expression of potential living in a winning (satisfying) or losing (sabotaging) way. In discussing the Face Shapes method in this chapter, I'll list the winning and losing tendencies for each shape. As we go through the client histories in part II, "The Face in Stories," I'll point out the factors that help or hinder clients in trying to maximize their innate possibilities.

3. Every face has two sides. The right side (governed by the left side of the brain) reflects consciousness, logic, and the material world. The left (governed by the right side of the brain) is the side of the subconscious, idealism, creativity, and dreams. Who we are is an expression of that duality. To evaluate a person, I begin by taking in the entire face, as we all do when forming first impressions, but then I must examine each side separately.

4. The eyes and mouth are critical for interpretation. Other aspects of the face are important, of course, but the eyes and mouth have special significance. I consider them fundamental to face reading for two reasons: because they are the most flexible and dynamic features, constantly in motion and communicating, and because they have direct connections to the brain—the eyes though the optic, oculomotor, and trochlear, and abducens nerves, and the mouth through special nerve networks dedicated to its many functions.

Part III, "A Face-Reading Reference Guide," offers more detailed information on the eyes and mouth—their shape, size, positioning, and so on—as well as on the eyebrows and other features. But it's more effective to process the whole face first, with receptiveness and intuition, before zeroing in on such specifics.

Some Basics of Chinese Face Reading

Certain traditional methods of Chinese face reading are based on "zones" or "regions" of the face. The face reader looks for anomalies, like scars or discolorations, and interprets them based on their exact location and appearance. For example, a wart always represents a caged negative emotion, like anger, and its placement shows in which realm of life the trouble lies. A smooth, unmarked zone might indicate ease, comfort, and even luck in a certain situation. I don't normally analyze people using these methods, but sometimes I draw on them for extra information.

Three Zones Method
This method divides the face into thirds. The relative size of the zones—say, a high forehead and a nose and chin that are close together—may suggest particular personality traits, depending on who is doing the reading.

1. **Zone 1, the Celestial Zone,** which is also associated with young adulthood, ages fifteen to thirty, stretches from the hairline to the eyebrows.
2. **Zone 2, the Zone of the Will or the Human Zone,** which is also associated with midlife, ages thirty to fifty, stretches from the eyebrows to the bottom of the nose.
3. **Zone 3, the Earthly Zone or the Zone of Age,** which is associated with life beyond age fifty, stretches from the bottom of the nose to the chin.

Eight Regions Method

All the regions in this method appear above the nose and leave out the mouth entirely. The regions are not as easy to describe, but some approximations follow:

1. **Region of Life,** the most important region, lies above the creases of the eyelids and stretches up to the eyebrows.
2. **Region of Drive (Determination**) is the temples (recessed temples indicate lack of drive).
3. **Region of Career** lies at the center of the forehead.
4. **Region of Prosperity** is the nose.
5. **Region of Friendship** lies in the center of the forehead, just below the hairline.
6. **Region of Parents** lies at the outer edges of the forehead, stretching from the temples to the hairline.
7. **Region of Health and Power** stretches from the inside corners of the eyes to the bridge of the nose.
8. **Region of Love** stretches around the outer edges of the eyes, especially encompassing the outer corners and lower eyelids.

Palaces of Luck Method

This method is more comprehensive and divides the face into twelve realms of life called the Twelve Palaces of Luck. The palaces, which correspond to the twelve houses of the Chinese zodiac, reveal what a person's fortune will be in realms such as career, love, health, and prosperity. What the palaces are, where they lie, and what they signify can vary, depending on where the master trained or his school of thought. The palaces can also be interpreted differently to address a client's particular questions.

The Twelve Palaces system bears comparison with the Personality Regions diagram that appears in part III, "A Face-Reading

Reference Guide," which is based on an Aristotelian classification of the regions of the face as they relate to personality.

As with other zone theories, "flaws" such as scars, moles, and lines appearing in the palaces require interpretation. I generally use this method of analysis and prediction only if people ask for it. Here's one version of the Twelve Palaces of Luck:

1. Palace of the Career, Kaun Lu Kung: This palace, which lies at the center of the forehead, governs both work and lasting friendship, especially with influential people. If the area is smooth and clear, you're probably popular and possess the magnetism and charm to attract the love support of well-placed friends. Uneven skin tone, moles, and scars in the area suggest that you'll face obstacles in work and friendship. You're probably destined to repeat the same lessons over and over but must remain determined and push toward your goals.

2. Palace of Movement and Travel, Ch'ien I Kung: This palace, which lies at the outer edges of the forehead and includes the temples, governs both your literal travels and your passage through life. If the temples aren't swollen or sunken and have no flaws, travel and exploration are favored and you might expect a smooth life path. If the temples are swollen or sunken or have moles or scars, you may be challenged on your journey though life and must be alert to potential difficulties, like accidents in your physical travels.

3. Palace of the Brothers, Hsiung Ti Kung: This palace, which lies just above the eyebrows and relates to their length and shape, governs not just relations with literal siblings but also with the "brothers" that life gives you. The state of your eyebrows describes what these brothers are like, your relationship with them, and how likely you are to lose them.

4. Palace of Life, Min Kung: This palace, which lies between the eyes, governs your emotional life. A clear, evenly colored area suggests stability in relationships, with enough time and inspiration to enjoy them. Prominent lines and other flaws indicate a bumpy emotional life, a burdened heart, and challenges with loved ones.

5. Palace of Health or Disease, Chi O Kung: This palace, which lies on the shaft of the nose, below the bridge, governs the overall state of your health. Even skin tone and lack of moles, scars, and the like suggest that you're in good shape and have little to fear, healthwise.

6. Palace of Prosperity, Ts'ai Dai Kung: This palace, which encompasses the tip of the nose, governs material success. The more well-formed—straighter, less curved or kinked—and unflawed the area is, the more likely you are to be blessed with wealth. Good form also indicates that you're responsible for your own efforts and that you believe in yourself. Flaws and discolorations represent the challenges life gives you, and if you have them, you should cultivate the strength to overcome them.

7. Palace of the House and Farm, T'ien Chai Kung: This palace, which lies above the crease of the upper eyelid, stretching to below the brow, governs your home life. If the area is unblemished and evenly colored, you can expect good fortune in your home. Any blemish warns of challenges, such as the challenge of poverty.

8. Palace of Man and Woman, Nan Nu Kung: This palace, which lies just below the eyes, on the lower lid, governs the family life. An unblemished, evenly colored area suggests harmony and indicates that any problems that arise will be resolved quickly. Scars, moles, and discolorations warn of discord.

9. Palace of Spouse and Lover, Ch'i Ch'ien Kung: This palace, which lies at the sides of the cheeks, governs the love life, whether in or outside marriage. A clear, smooth area suggests harmony in love, while blemishes and discolorations imply conflict or lack of love.

10. **Palace of the Servant, Nu P'u Kung:** This palace, which lies at the crease between the lips and the chin, governs relations between friends of equal stature. The term *servant* refers to serving friendship, not to serving another person. The area's appearance addresses questions of trust and mistrust, whether you value the opinions of others, and so on. Lines and other flaws may suggest that you are tactless or unnecessarily make enemies.

11. **Palace of Luck and Virtue, Fu Te Kung:** This palace is not associated with any fixed point of the face but related to facial expressions. The kind of expressions you make and how they are revealed show how your luck is developing.

12. **Palace of the Face, Hsiang Mao Kung:** This palace, too, is not a fixed point, but an index of the face, a summary of what other points reveal, offering a description of your overall outlook.

Narrative Method

A more philosophical method of analysis is based on the structures of the face and depends on the storytelling skill of the face reader. The client's features are metaphors and the way they relate creates a plotline. For example, the chin is the South Mountain and the forehead the North Mountain, while the softer features might be rivers. The reader looks at the "landscape" of the face and constructs a narrative explaining the client's personality.

Five Elements Methods

Some important face-reading methods incorporate the Five Elements or Five Phases (Wu Xing), which are metaphors for the fundamental energies of the universe. The Five Elements are

Wood, Fire, Earth, Metal, and Water. Deeply embedded in Chinese culture, the Five Elements theory is a way to organize and understand the world.

Thus, every aspect of life—mental, physical, and spiritual—is assigned to a category based on its energy: parts of the body, the properties of medicinal drugs, notes and pitches in music, martial arts moves, colors, the points on a compass, the seasons of the year, the weather, the time of day, the roles people play in family and society, and more. There are charts showing the aspects of life and qualities associated with each element. For example, regarding the colors, Wood is associated with green, Fire with red, Earth with yellow, Metal with white, and Water with blue and black.

Part of the point of the Five Elements is to explain how different aspects of life interact, which might be in a "generating" (positive and supportive) or "overcoming" (negative and destructive) way. The established sequences of interaction are

- *Generating:* Wood fuels Fire, Fire creates Earth (ash), Earth contains Metal (ore), Metal carries Water (buckets, pipes), and Water feeds Wood (trees).
- *Overcoming:* Fire melts Metal, Metal penetrates Wood (axes, saws, nails), Wood separates Earth (tree roots breaking up soil and rock), Earth absorbs Water, and Water quenches Fire.

Usually, the goal in working with the Five Elements is to find balance. Here are some highly simplified examples of how face-reading systems might accomplish this:

Feng Shui. People's surroundings can affect them in either a supportive or destructive way. For example, certain people flourish in certain cities. London is a Metal city, which would be supportive to someone with a Water nature but less so to someone with a Wood nature. New York and Hong are Fire cities, which would sustain an Earth person but be less comfortable for a Metal person.

People stuck in inhospitable places have to counteract their environments by increasing the supportive elements in their lives, so a Metal person in a Fire city would resist being consumed by bringing in Water elements to quench the Fire, as well as Earth elements for support. By the same token, a Fire person living in a Fire city might want to strengthen the other elements in life to avoid burning too hot.

Personality. The starting point for facial analysis might be the personality traits associated with each element:

- Wood: idealism, spontaneity, and curiosity
- Fire: passion and intensity
- Earth: amiability and honesty
- Metal: intuition and rationality
- Water: resourcefulness, wit, and erudition

A look at how people interact—again, this is simplistic because there are many potential mitigating factors—might go like this: a person with a Wood nature might be an inspiring partner for one with Fire nature but feel criticized by the rational Metal person and, in turn, offend the good-natured Earth person. An intense Fire person could stimulate the easygoing Earth person, but both might be a bad match for a Water person—for Fire because the Water would quash its passions and for Water because the energy of Earth would slow and muddy its flow. Even those who are well matched need to stay in balance—so, for example, a Wood person should be careful about giving too much when feeding the Fire.

How does a face reader determine a person's nature? The shape and appearance of the features are categorized as well. For example, a flexible, pointed mouth would be associated with a Fire nature, but in the same person, a forehead with lots of straight, unbroken lines, would suggest a Wood nature. The face reader would then add up the number of Fire, Wood, and other element features to determine which element dominates the face.

Many of us, of course, have more than one dominant element, which makes face reading—and the effort to balance the Five Elements—as much an art as a science.

Face Shapes Method

A method that I'll feature prominently in this book involves the shape of the face. The face shape offers an outline of the personality—it's sort of an introduction. Interestingly, in Asia, Mien Shiang practitioners speak of some thirty different shapes, but in the West we deal with a basic eight to ten. The reason is that, given the intermingling of people over the millennia since the categories were established, Western faces usually combine two or more shapes. Among my clients, I'd estimate that only a quarter to a third have one dominant face shape. About 45 percent have two, which might appear side by side (one shape on the left and the other on the right), vertically stacked (one shape on the upper face and one on the lower), or in other configurations. Combination faces were relatively rare in ancient China, but the tradition does acknowledge them.

About 15 to 20 percent of the faces I read combine three different face shapes. The most commonly observed mixes have been assigned their own categories—the Dragon face, for example, combines Jade, King, and Fire. Very few people—maybe 5 to 10 percent of those I see—combine four or more face shapes. This unusual category is called Master of Masks.

Part III, "A Face-Reading Reference Guide," goes into detail about the different face shapes and the traits associated with them. But it's important to remember that face shape is just the beginning. There are many more variables to consider in assessing a face, which appear in an immeasurable number of combinations. Every individual on the planet—and hence, every visage—is unique. In effect, there are 7.6 billion types of faces.

The face shapes we'll cover here are:

- ***Jade face***—somewhat heart-shaped with a wider forehead and a rounded chin. They tend to be open-minded and appreciative of beauty but can err on the side of timidity and indecision.

- ***King face***—angular with a strong jawline and prominent chin, cheekbones, and forehead. They tend to be strong, decisive, and protective of the weak but can err on the side of aggressiveness and dogmatism.

- *Fire face*—somewhat triangle-shaped with a wider forehead and pointed chin. They tend to be passionate and vibrant but can err on the side of impatience, distractability, and self-involvement.

- *Tree face*—long and wide, often with a U-shaped line running from the mouth to beneath the chin. They tend to be trustworthy and comforting but err on the side of being stuck in one place, resistant to change, and emotionally disconnected.

- *Moon face*—big and round, in a circular head. They tend to be great communicators, colorful, and loyal but err on the side of passivity and lack of discipline.

- **Bucket face**—flowerpot-shaped, with a square chin and sides angled up to a wider forehead. They tend to be creative, pragmatic, and inspiring to others but err on the side of feeling stuck without a muse or a leader.

- **Mountain face**—pear-shaped, fuller at the jowls than at the backward-sloping forehead. They tend to be resilient, generous loners, and late bloomers but can err on the side of procrastination and being emotionally withdrawn.

- **Ground Face (or Earth face)**—shaped like a pyramid with a lopped-off top, wider at the jawline than the forehead. They tend to be dynamic movers and shakers but can err on the side of overconfidence and bullying.

- **_Iron face_**—flat, shaped like a squared-off Moon face. They are unflappable, rational, and loyal but can err on the side of sluggishness and fatalism.

- **_Wall face_**—broader than it is long, a relatively rare shape in the West. They are reliable, highly capable, and practical but can err on the side of self-involvement and emotional disconnection.

Some Combination Faces. Left to right: Jade King Face, Jade Moon Face, Fire Tree Face

As we go through part II, "The Face in Stories," I'll discuss what the interplay of face shapes, features, expressions, and other factors reveal about our lives—from our personalities, Life Purposes, talents, and paths to success to our health, love, and relationships—and even what others might think of us.

You and I—and everyone else in the world—have written autobiographies. Our stories are published on our faces. We can find enlightenment in those stories through the art and science of face reading.

PART II

The Face in Stories

5

Personality and Character

How does your autobiography begin? A face reader would say that it's outlined at birth—not in the sense that your life is preordained but because you're born with certain attributes, which will show up in your features, as well as certain talents and a Life Purpose, as discussed in chapter 6. We call this essence, this architecture of your life, your "personality."

The face shapes discussed in chapter 4 are rough sketches of different personalities. As we grow out of our baby faces, a face shape emerges (and over the course of our lives, perhaps a second or third). Our fixed features—the eyes and mouth especially, but also the nose, ears, eyebrows, and hair—develop in a unique configuration that defines our personality, or the core of who we are.

When we live authentically, we're expressing our inborn personality. Naturally, almost no one does that perfectly. When we use our innate strengths to achieve our Life Purpose, we're living in a "winning" way. When we don't—or when we default to our inherent weaknesses—we're living in a "losing" way. Most of us flip back and forth between these states of being.

Over the course of our lives, our personality gets an overlay of "character." Character is not inborn but develops through outside influences—our culture, environment and life situation, families, education, spouses and friends, even small and major life experiences. Face readers construe character from our nonfixed features, notably our facial expressions, which are generated by the brain but can be controlled.

Even more telling are microexpressions, because they appear automatically and for only a fraction of a second, which we'll discuss in chapter 7. When I consult on police investigations or on corporate hiring decisions, often I only glance at personality traits. Instead, I concentrate on cues like behavior, gestures, and facial expressions, including microexpressions, which convey character. I don't need to weigh the more global, subconscious forces of personality, but rather the acute sensibility of the person—who he or she is right in that moment.

Ideally, our character would align with our personality, but, again, the best that most of us can achieve is some overlap. When there's little connection between character and personality, we're often depressed, frustrated, or even aggressive. The more personality and character are in sync, the greater the integrity and fulfillment we experience.

Fortunately, character can be developed. In fact, my German master put me through a rather intensive crash course in character development. It wasn't a punishing or judgmental exercise but rather an effort to help me expand to match the potential he saw in my personality. During my apprenticeship, he'd seen that I craved knowledge and had a strong bent for detection and analysis. Though these are good traits in a face reader, he wanted more from me.

We were sitting in a lovely lakeside restaurant in a German enclave of Italy. The next day, his other students would arrive, so it was just the two of us. "Eric," the master said, "you know what one of your biggest problems is? You don't communicate. You can't talk to people."

"What?" I was shocked. "I was a radio announcer. I did public relations. I managed a huge staff."

"Yes, but those were jobs. You were trying to reach goals. You're interested in your goals but not in people."

I kept arguing, until he said, "You see the couple at that table? They're speaking German. Go over there, introduce yourself, and talk to them."

"Are you kidding? Who would do that? That's crazy."

"Well, if you won't do it, I will."

He got up and said hello, then wound up joining them for dinner. I sat there alone, picking over my spaghetti. Finally, after coffee and warm good-byes, they left and he returned to our table.

"Well, that was interesting," he reported. "They're both doctors. They're visiting their daughter, who's studying in Milan, and decided to take a day trip. . . ."

He went on, talking about what they'd seen and recommended, as if nothing extraordinary had happened. I waited for the punchline, his lesson.

"From now on, it will be your turn," the master told me. "When our group goes out to eat, you're not allowed at our table. Instead, you have to find someone else in the restaurant to sit with and talk to, just as I did."

Imagine my horror. But for the next five months, I did it. My master and the others would order dinner, while I approached strangers, saying, "Hello, I'm Eric. I hate to bother you, but my master wants me to practice communicating with you. . . ."

It was humbling, to say the least.

I got every conceivable reaction, from kindness to scorn and outright laughter. In Switzerland, people thought I was psycho. In Bavaria, the attitude was, "The more the merrier! Have a beer."

Much as I dreaded every encounter, I began to grasp what it meant to interact without goals. My mantra became, "There's nothing I have to work for in this conversation. I just have to be present and see where it goes."

The exercise did fill out my character, teaching me to be still and let my intuition guide me. I wouldn't recommend such a trial by fire to someone else. But my master devised this particular discipline for me to awaken my capacity to perceive and connect with others, both as a novice face reader and a human being.

The stories in this chapter will illustrate how personality is expressed and how it might be lived most effectively.

A Baby's Teaching

Personality is inborn, face readers believe, while character develops with life experience. This principle was dramatically illustrated

when a couple consulted me to settle a dispute. The husband, in his fifties, headed a top law firm. His wife, twenty years younger, was more artistic, a former ballerina who played the violin. Physically, too, they were opposites. He was a big man with a middle-aged belly, while she was very thin, with the gaunt look and perfect carriage of a supermodel.

They'd been arguing about their year-old daughter. Although the child could speak only a handful of words, each parent had mapped out her future. The mother planned to enroll her in pre-ballet at age four, as well as lessons on the quarter violin, and then have the child attend her own alma mater, a chic private girls' school. The father insisted on early language training, to make the child multilingual, then a rigorous prep school education, with an eye to a legal career and, ultimately, leadership at his firm.

They wanted me to read the baby's face, to see which plan should prevail. But how? Most babies have the same features: a round or oval face, smooth skin, full lips, and prominent eyes with large pupils. That's why I never read children under the age of seven and try to stick to post-adolescents. The couple kept pushing until I agreed to try, though I warned, "I'm not going to lie. I may see nothing at all and the reading will be over in five minutes."

As I studied the child's face, the words of one of my Chinese masters came to mind: "It is written on the forehead." Babies are born with distinct personalities, as any parent can attest, and with lines on their foreheads that tend to disappear in the first two years. Because the muscles of the face are connected so directly to the brain, some face readers believe that these lines can offer a hint of inborn traits, before culture, the will of others, and experience can exert influence.

This baby's forehead had a lot of very fine, horizontal lines in a band near the hairline, away from the brows. Normally lines close to the brows reflect the person's connection to the material world; the mid-forehead lines relate to the ego and a person's self-love; and higher lines indicate spirituality and imagination. This child did have a faint, winglike line above each eyebrow, signifying intuition and instinct, and the beginnings of a vertical line centered above the bridge of the nose, which is called the hanging needle. The hanging needle indicates drive, self-direction (or possible stubbornness), and leadership.

Putting all these clues together, I was able to offer a glimpse of who the baby might become. "I don't see a corporate warrior or a physical being like a dancer in this face," I said. "Your baby is an idealist, who will have humanitarian concerns. Maybe she'll be a healer. Maybe she'll dedicate her life to saving the planet. Maybe she'll do creative work aimed at helping others."

The two fought back on that. "A lawyer helps others," the father said. "Saving the planet is a battle waged in the courts, not on the streets."

"Not everyone's driven and cutthroat like you," the mother replied. "You want to fast-track her into law before she can even read. To play an instrument, you need to start young—no later than five or six. The same with ballet. To do well in the arts, she'll have to get serious early. She'll never catch up if we wait."

As they quarreled, they forgot that I was there. Unwittingly, I'd given them new ammunition in an old war. "Hold it," I said. "You're not listening. Neither of you owns this child and has the right to control her life. What's more, I can see that this child won't let you. There are signs"—the lines of instinct and intuition—"that she'll be very good at playing the two of you against each other. Meanwhile, she'll be determined"—the hanging needle—"to find her own path. If you each keep struggling to cast her in your own image, you'll push her away as well as undermine your marriage. Do you want that?"

"It seems to me that this baby was sent to you not as a battle-ground but as a bridge, to bind you together as loving partners and loving parents."

They weren't happy, but I felt that I'd made my case as an advocate for the baby. So it was gratifying when, two days later, the father came to see me. "I understand your point," he told me. "I myself was forced into law school by my father. I've worked hard and had great success, but I feel that I missed my calling. I can't speak for my wife, who's still stewing, but I can promise you that my daughter will get to make the choices I couldn't. Thank you for reminding me."

Eyes Without a Face

In February 2017, I was invited to speak at the World Government Summit in Dubai, a gathering of international groups like the World Bank and the United Nations Educational, Scientific, and Cultural Organization (UNESCO). Other speakers included the prime minister of Japan, who gave the keynote address, and disrupters like the Uber founders. What an honor!

At the meet-and-greet session after the talk, I was approached by a woman swathed head to toe in a black burka. Only her eyes were visible. "I wish you could read my face," she said. "But I suppose it's impossible."

It was a challenge. But instead of calling the eyes the windows to the soul, we should call them the windows of the brain, since they're directly connected via the optic nerve. So there was a lot of information I could glean from her eyes alone.

One obvious clue was the dark circles under her eyes. "I guess you haven't been sleeping much," I said. "Not just last night but over the past few weeks. You've also been doing too much in your

waking hours, because I can see that you're exhausted. Maybe you've even had a touch of the flu."

That surprised her—she had just recovered from the flu—but dark circles always signify deficient energy, usually from sleeplessness, recent illness, or depleted iron in the body. The outer edge of the dark circles had a reddish violet tinge, typically a sign of excess cortisol production, due to stress.

My biggest tipoff that she was exhausted was the sclera (the white part) visible below the iris of her eyes. Usually, the iris touches both the upper and lower eyelids, but the sclera can peep out below the iris from fatigue and depletion or, in some people, intense preoccupation.

I couldn't judge how old she was, but she had lines below her eyes, possibly from age, that suggested connective-tissue weakness and, because her eyelids were slightly swollen, potential weakness of the kidneys and bladder. She also had three lines across the bridge of her nose. Horizontal lines there indicate back problems, and the higher the lines appear, the higher up the back the trouble lies. Hers made me think that her neck was painful and stiff, possibly from tension. "Why, yes it is," she told me. "Everything you've said is true."

By then she was eager to hear about her personality. When I met her, the first thing I spotted was a mole between her eye and her temple. A mole in that position is the sign of the traveler. If it appears on the right side, it shows that you're impelled to reach outward, to engage with the world. On the left, it suggests that you're more inclined to travel inward, through the emotions, that you may be melancholic or a daydreamer. Hers was on the left. She confirmed that she had an introspective nature.

"You're very determined and bold," I went on. "Being strong-minded in a culture where women have lots of constraints must be a challenge."

"Yes, we have our limitations," she said. "But how can you tell I'm determined?"

She had the eyes of the jaguar, I explained. They angled upward at the outer corners. Cartoon and comic book characters—either heroes or villains—have exaggerated versions of such eyes, which suggest dynamism. Cartoon characters with eyes that slant downward at the outer corners tend to be sad sacks, weary, broken down, or passive.

"That suggests that you're a person of action, bold and strong-willed," I told her. "You seek out what you want, rather than wait for it to come to you. You're expressive, but also intuitive and receptive. Your pupils show me that. They're large, suggesting that you're imaginative and creative. You must have dozens of dreams at night. Your heart is big, too, which makes you vulnerable, easily wounded by other people's words."

When I finished, she wanted a full reading, but to show me her face, she had to ask her husband. She called him, but he didn't pick up. "Well," she said, "I'll take that as yes." Westerners perceive women in traditional garb as passive, meek, and fearful. But here was a vivid example—not an unusual one, I've found, during my time in the Middle East—of determination in action.

The Perfect Host

Some people seem innately likable. Other people flock to them because they feel instantly accepted and welcomed. These qualities may not always add up to a talent for deep friendship, but they are a definite gift. "There must be something in their faces that attracts us," a friend observed. "What makes them so magnetic?"

We were talking about a French restaurant owner in Bangkok, whose place was always mobbed. The food was good enough—above average—but it was far from the best around. We'd just had dinner there specifically so I could check him out. When I met the host, without even talking much, I could feel his warmth.

"Can I snap your picture?" my friend asked. The genial host agreed, which gave me a photo to analyze further.

His forehead had many straight, unbroken horizontal lines, which was noteworthy. Most people have at least three, with the bottom line representing the material world, the center line corresponding to the self or the ego, and the top line relating to idealism and spiritual concerns. Many people also have so-called instinct lines, arcs above each eyebrow that form with lots of *aha!* moments, when they literally or figuratively raise their eyebrows, as if to say, "Got it!"

The more lines on the forehead, the more complex the personality and the broader the person's range of interests. Unbroken lines indicate that the person is in relative balance and completes what is started. So people with lots of unbroken lines have many genuine interests, suggesting that they will welcome any topic you raise or, if you have little to say, will have enough material to engage you. Such a person has the potential to put you at ease.

The host's eyes were another important key to his appeal. Rather than point straight toward the temples, the outer corners slanted downward, like a comic book character's. In comic books, people with downturned eyes are often victims because such eyes announce, "I'm nonthreatening; I'm a peaceful personality." But when accompanied by a warm smile, they convey affection and sympathy. They made his guests feel comfortable and embraced.

He had a mustache and a bearded chin, with clean-shaven cheeks, indicating that he was a responsible, take-charge person. His wide mouth with upturned corners softened his authoritative look, indicating that he was ethical and trustworthy. Even his hairline, with a slight widow's peak, suggested reliability, implying, "I'm independent and don't need much from others, but I'm there for anyone who needs me."

"Wow," my friend said, "that's quite an endorsement. Evidently people intuit all this and adore him. Is there anything negative you see?"

"We don't judge faces as positive and negative or good and bad," I said. "Just in terms of potential for living in a winning or losing way. Looking at a photo, I can't ascertain his microexpressions, which would be more revealing. But I can vaguely see one area of possible concern—his love life."

He had the nose of a connoisseur, large in proportion to his face and thickened and wide at the nostrils. The tip of the nose connects via the nervous system to the stomach. His was bulbous, suggesting digestive stress due to excess. Clearly, he was a pleasure seeker, which might extend to seeking out love affairs.

My friend laughed. "Maybe so, but you don't know his wife. She's tough. I'd hate to be him if she ever caught him cheating. She'd probably go after him with a razor."

"Oh no," I said. "Luckily, I can't see what he's really up to. I can only spot potential. And admire the fact that he's in a line of work that complements his personality so well."

The De-Energizer

People like the "Perfect Host" buoy us, but there are personalities that actively drag us down, sometimes without our knowing it. One of my health clients, whom I'd urged to slow down and relax, encountered this on a trip to India. By videoconference he reported that he'd taken my advice and was doing a yoga and meditation course at a well-known retreat center. "I'm working with this Canadian guy who seems great. But, man, I am so exhausted after every class."

"That's probably because you've never tried yoga before. You're using muscles you never knew you had."

"Maybe," he said. "Everyone says I should feel strong and energized, but that hasn't happened yet."

"Good luck," I told him. "Let me know how it goes."

A week later he e-mailed: "That class is murder. I really like the teacher, but I'm still bone-tired."

"Send me the guy's picture," I wrote back. I was curious to see what his face would reveal about the way he was working my client.

In the photo, the teacher's broad shoulders and thin, muscled arms looked mismatched. He appeared to be close to sixty, with white hair and a sculpted handsomeness. His face mixed Jade and King elements, an appealing combination known as the "warm-hearted warrior." That was probably one reason my client liked him. Another, no doubt, was the tension visible in his body, which echoed my client's own restless nature. The impression of body tension was confirmed by a slight protuberance of the teacher's eyes. I wondered if that restiveness had drawn him to yoga.

The teacher had the half-lidded eyes of a dreamer and the Jade face's seductive gaze. His mouth was wide, suggesting that he was an effective, even influential communicator. His lips were average size but slightly unbalanced, tilted lower on the right side. The imbalance implied that he played with words, whether for the benefit or deception of the listener.

His ears were unusual, too, with tops situated a few inches below his eyes. In babyhood, we have ears in that position, but in most people, by adulthood, the tops of the ears are at eye level. In Chinese face reading, low-placed ears indicate a calculating nature, especially the tendency to delay decisions while weighing every angle.

Between the teacher's eyebrows was a single vertical wrinkle, known as the hanging needle. It could signify dedication, deter-mination, and focus or, on the flip side, single-minded stubborn-ness and disregard for others. I couldn't tell which from a photo, nor could I tell whether the drive it implied was a hangover from the past—a trait cultivated in some prior business career—or a current influence. Judging by my client's exhaustion, I had to sus-pect that the teacher still had a hard-driving disposition.

So far, I could conclude that he was a restless personality, slow to make decisions, very calculating, and highly persuasive or in-fluential. But when I considered the sides of his face separately, I was blown away. Covering the right side and looking at the left, his material and analytic side, I saw the perfect Jade face—oval and beautiful, with a soulful eye—marked with just a few wrinkles. But when I looked only at his right, emotional side, his face was spooky, almost frightening.

The most startling feature was his right eye. Usually, the iris, the colored part of the eye, is centered in the white part, the sclera. But in the teacher's right eye, the iris was so close to the inner corner that only a hint of sclera was visible. That gave his half-closed right eyelid a shape that, in Chinese tradition, represents an ancient knife, pointed at the material side of his face. It strongly suggested a cruel nature.

Looking at the right side of his face, I remembered reading a story about an old man living in a castle, who would invite young villagers to dinner. They'd all vie for the honor of sitting next to him, and as they ate he'd tell stories about his life. But as one visitor studied the family portraits on the walls, the painted faces contorted and turned devilish. With that, she realized the old man's secret: that he invited young people in order to steal their youth. His guests would suffer early deaths, but he'd go on living as long as he sucked energy from those he lured to the castle.

Was that how the teacher functioned? By feeding off the students' energy? What I could see from a photo was limited, of course, but the potential seemed real. There are people who, because of their influence, can manipulate us emotionally in ways that bolster their egos while diminishing ours.

My client had viscerally experienced the teacher as such a person. He didn't know what to make of it, and neither did I until I saw the photo supporting his feeling. One of the great benefits of face reading is that it helps us develop our powerful, built-in detection system—our intuition—and also helps us trust what we sense. So I could confidently tell my client, "I doubt that you're still exhausted because you're out of shape. This teacher might seem charismatic, but your body is sending you a message. From what I see in the photo, I think you should pay attention and switch classes. There are teachers who will lift you up, not wear you down."

Jealousy

One day, I got a frantic call from London. One of my clients, a warmhearted Indian woman with a Polish husband, was in a strange predicament. She'd taken pity on a young woman they knew from the yoga center to which they were devoted.

The woman had been crying in the locker room. "My boyfriend kicked me out," she'd said. "I don't know where to go or what to do."

"I felt so bad," my client told me. "She's barely twenty and from Hong Kong, alone in a foreign city. She looked so lost. I invited her to stay with us a couple days to sort things out. But now it's been two weeks. And while I'm at the office, she's home with my husband."

She worked long hours in finance, while her husband, a professor, had a flexible schedule. "I can't stand the thought of them alone together," she said.

"You know I've read him and don't see him as a cheater."

I was reminding her that, in the past, she'd had bouts of jealous fear.

"Maybe I'm crazy, but I have a bad feeling about her. Please read her and tell me what you think."

She reposted an Instagram picture. All I could think was, "Wow!" The young woman was Chinese and stunningly beautiful, with fine bones, porcelain skin, and soulful eyes. Her black hair, streaked with auburn, was adorned with a rosy camellia behind her ear. The close-up of her face and bare shoulders was shot on a balcony overlooking blue water with a tethered boat—dreamy, soft-focus, and romantic.

I could see why my client, almost twice her age, was jealous.

"Why don't you tell her to leave?" I said.

"I don't want to overreact."

I always remind my students that no face is symmetrical. We might start by considering the face as a whole, but to read a personality, we have to examine each side separately. The left, as I've noted, is the side of the subconscious and emotions, while the right represents logic and the material world.

Right away, I noticed imbalances in her face. The right side was oval, delicate Jade, but she had the pointed chin of a Fire face. On the left she had some King face elements, notably an eye that looked more deep-set than the other. Combined, these three shapes form a Dragon face, which is a face with tremendous power.

Studying her individual features, I was struck by her mouth. Her shapely lips suggested skill at communicating and entertaining, but they were uneven. On the right, they sloped gracefully to the corner of the mouth; but on the left, emotional side, they stopped short. The thin, lipless segment connecting them to the corner of the mouth signified secret feelings. Her hair swept down the left side of her face, covering half her eyebrow and the corner of her eye, reinforcing the sense of concealment. Her more deep-set left eye was also narrowed—the eye of a fighter—with the squint of calculation.

Covering the left side of the woman's visage, on the right you'd see the guileless, trusting, open-eyed, open-minded, and fragile beauty of a Jade face; but covering the right side of her face and seeing only the left, you'd judge her to be a shrewd, almost fierce-looking schemer. The camellia behind her right ear seemed placed, perhaps subconsciously, to draw attention away from her conniving left side and highlight her soft, sensitive nature.

"You're intuiting something real," I told my client. "Not that she's seducing your husband—that I doubt—but she's definitely not as weak and helpless as she seems. I think that she's a chiseler who'll take advantage as long as you let her. I'd sit down with her today—not tomorrow—and set a deadline for her to leave."

My client did, and the woman cleared out by the appointed date. "I feel so much better," she said. "Thank you for confirming that my suspicions made sense. You know, she actually did seduce my husband, though not for what I thought. When I told him she was leaving, he was shocked. 'Why? Where will the poor girl go? It hasn't been long. Shouldn't we give her at least a month?'"

I laughed. "The longer she stayed, the harder it would be to get her out."

"Definitely. He was getting so protective. But I told him that you promised she'd be fine."

The Soft-Hearted Fighter

Faces often reveal the dynamics of the relationship of couples, suggesting imbalances that might be addressed. But as this story shows, an imbalance can be the factor that unites a couple and makes the relationship a success.

I was working in Thailand at a health spa—a place less for pampering than for healing through Western and Traditional Chinese Medicine, along with massage, homeopathy, and other modes of alternative therapy. The Asian practitioners usually asked me to consult on their diagnoses and encouraged me to offer my services to other therapists.

An American nutritionist I approached wasn't interested. She was polite enough but didn't make eye contact and, when she spoke, the left corner of her mouth turned down—obvious signs of a brushoff. But she picked up her phone and showed me a photo

of her boyfriend, a big, burly blond guy in shoulder pads and a football jersey. "What can you tell me about him?" she asked.

I was immediately struck by how different they looked. She, a small, wiry brunette, was at least a foot shorter. But even without talking to her or studying her face, I had no doubt that she dominated the relationship.

Her boyfriend's face projected an almost childlike tenderness, in sharp contrast to his jock image. His hair was curly and tousled; his eyes were large and shining, with big pupils and long lashes. He had a wide, welcoming mouth with full lips and, at the corners, little wrinkles that suggested frequent laughter.

Though I couldn't clearly see his cheeks, which were smooth and pink, I thought I detected dimples. The cheeks are the "pillows of power," in the Chinese view, so dimples, indentations in the cheeks, connote softness. They don't limit the power but temper its expression. It's hard to imagine a hard-driving CEO or a commanding leader with dimples. It was surprising to see them in a football player.

I surmised from his face that his role on the team was probably that of a morale builder or a unifier—the guy known for his charm, wit, and passion for the game, rather than his fierce prowess. In a movie, he would more likely play the romantic lead, like Hugh Grant or George Clooney, than a he-man like Arnold Schwarzenegger. My opinion was confirmed by one especially telling sign, a large mole on his Adam's apple. That placement, according to Chinese face readers, "turns the fighter into a dreamer" (or turns a woman, traditionally a dreamer, into a fighter).

When I told his girlfriend my impressions, she was stunned. "Yes, that's all true," she said. "At first, I thought I wanted—and was getting—a 'manly man,' but now I appreciate that he's so kind, reliable, and honest. He wears his emotions on his sleeve. He knows I love travel and has given me the freedom to work in Asia for a while. The very things I never realized I needed are the reasons I love him."

The Woman and the Moon

Just as we don't see Arnold Schwarzenegger as a romantic lead, we wouldn't cast Sharon Stone or Heidi Klum in a stay-at-home, baking-pies maternal role. These women have King faces, which means that they're leaders, which is not to say that they're unfeminine or don't make good mothers. As always, it's a question of finding balance.

Usually, in women a King face appears in some softening combination, but one of my Asian clients was a rare pure specimen.

She had the classic angular face with prominent cheekbones, chin, and forehead; strong jaws; deep-set eyes with small pupils; and the single horizontal line across one cheek known as a "power wrinkle."

She even had a stereotypical King lifestyle. She was the tough CEO of a company, muscular and lean from her daily workouts, and a gourmet, with a hankering for steak. She was an over-achiever in every realm but one. "We're trying so hard to have a child," she told me. "But it's not working."

"Tell me about your husband," I said.

He was a musician who played the piano at hotel bars. Though he was successful, he was the opposite of driven. His photo showed that he was a Moon face, having a round, soft visage with smooth skin and no hint of stubble; full lips on a wide mouth; large, gleaming eyes and big pupils—the perfect image of a follower. They probably had a good relationship because they both loved pleasure—good food, love, the arts—and he preferred being passive. He was happy to have her craft their fun-loving life together.

But even in that she pushed hard. She started work at seven in the morning and got home by six, in time to drive her husband to his gigs. When he finished playing in the wee hours, she was always there to pick him up. "Why?" I asked. "You barely have a chance to sleep."

"I'm afraid that he'll meet some woman," she confessed. "The bars are full of them."

Her husband never had a chance to breathe, though he no doubt liked her possessiveness. He certainly tolerated behavior that many would find stifling. "I don't see him leaving you," I said. "He'd have to take the initiative, for one thing, which seems unlikely. He's in paradise with you running his life."

But for her, all that pushing, controlling, obsessing, and so on took a toll. "You act like a warrior, " I told her. "The way you eat, exercise, and work, as well as worry about your husband, is exhausting you. It's boosting your testosterone, when you need estrogen. A body that's embattled can't stop fighting and get pregnant."

What I was saying may not have sounded politically correct, but it resonated. "Give your husband some space." I said. "He can take a cab home. Let him take charge now and then. You're treating him—and letting him behave—like the kid you want to have. If he's going to be a father, he needs the chance to start acting like a man."

It would be hard to shift gears in their normal routine, I suspected. So I encouraged her to take a two- or three-week vacation with her husband, with nothing to achieve—just to concentrate on each other. The idea shocked her. "Two or three weeks! I've never taken more than a couple of days off in a row!"

But they did head off to a Thai resort. A year or so later, I was thrilled to get a happy letter and a photo of the three of them.

A Beard's Tale

This story has a German spin, but it has resonance for every couple because it shows how a dominant partner's personality can, for better or worse, affect the other. It also reveals a little of the language of beards.

In some rural German states, a lot of men take pride in their beards, growing them long, trimming them into bold shapes—like two long points in front, with cheek sections curled at the ends to match the shape of an upturned mustache—and even entering

beard competitions. So I wasn't surprised that a rural man who came for a consultation had a lavishly styled white beard. Nor was I surprised that he was skeptical about face reading, since his own face was almost totally obscured. I suspected that a man with such a beard had the need to express himself—to be seen and heard by others—but didn't really want to be known and perhaps rarely sought to engage deeply on an emotional level.

That suggested to me that he was troubled by someone else. Since he wore a wedding ring, I surmised that it was his wife.

"I think your wife is exhausted," I told him. "She's not as creative and expressive as you are. She's more passive. But she supports you in every way."

He was stunned. "What do you know about my wife? How did you know she's having problems?"

"I see it in your beard," I said. "It draws every eye to you. When you're out with your wife, I'm sure she hangs back. You control every interaction. She's the second string in your relationship, but I think she's proud of you and loves you very much. Are you worried that she's gaining weight?"

"Yes," he said, dumbfounded.

I was guessing a little bit. But a woman with such an attention-seeking man will always be one of two things: putting on pounds or else scrawny and depleted.

"Well, you look to be in your sixties." I said. "If she's close to your age, she probably has diabetes. I suspect that she lives on carbohydrates and coffee—sugar and caffeine—which are the two big sources of energy. She needs energy because she invests all of hers in you. More than you ever give back."

All he could say was, "Wow." Then, to his credit, he asked, "What can I do?"

"First of all, be conscious that you're buoyed by your wife's energy. Don't always 'fill the room.' Step back and give her a

Facial Hair

A face covered with hair doesn't necessarily hinder a reading. Beards and mustaches are expressions of individuality that offer plenty of information. Here are some questions that I consider in deciphering their meaning.

What do they cover?

- A beard or overgrown mustache covering the mouth and lips implies keeping secrets and hiding emotions. Often, older men let their facial hair obscure their mouths as if to avoid discussing the past.
- Younger men tend to leave their upper lips exposed, so as to look masculine but communicative. Their beards are more for decoration than concealment.

What's the shape?

- Traditionally, rulers and sages, like druids and old Chinese masters, are depicted with pointed beards to suggest authority.
- Today, when fewer men grow full beards, modern versions like a "soul patch"—a little bit of hair below the lips—or a chin beard, with clean-shaven cheeks, are also declarations of power.
- Flourishes added to the shape of beards or sideburns express the wearer's sensitivity and, sometimes, a degree of passivity.

What's the length?

- A long beard, cut straight across the bottom, as you might see on an Amish man or an Arab leader, signifies connection to a higher cause, like a movement or a belief system. In effect, the straight cut acts like an extension or a widening of the chin, which is the seat of ideals.
- A long beard, cut round on the bottom, is more benevolent but, because it covers so much, lends an air of mystery. Santa Claus's

beard, for example, maintains his mythic status while showing him to be kindly.

- A short, closely trimmed beard covering the cheeks asserts masculinity, implying trustworthiness and capability. Men with baby faces or more feminine features often cultivate such beards.

- A few days' growth of hair marks the wearer as an iconoclast, one who resists routines and cherishes his freedom, including the freedom not to shave.

Perhaps the most eccentric kind of facial hair is the "fly," the little patch mustache worn by Charlie Chaplin and Robert Mugabe, but most strongly associated with Adolf Hitler. It covers the philtrum, the vertical crease running from the nose to the upper lip, which Greek face readers regarded as the seat of affection. Hiding that spot might indicate the lack of a philtrum, suggesting a person is incapable of affection, or a deep philtrum, reflecting intense emotionality. People who wear a "fly" tend to be private and asocial, though they may crave attention on the dais or screen. As Chaplin wrote in a preface to his autobiography, "There is a line of demarcation between oneself and the public. . . . There are things which if divulged to the public . . . my personality would disappear like the waters of the rivers that flow into the sea."

little space to breathe. Focus on what she enjoys, what makes her feel creative and fulfilled. Support her in pursuing those things. Encourage her to spend time with friends. Not only will your efforts help her, they will also enhance your relationship, making it more of a give-and-take than a one-way street."

Perhaps supporting his wife would also bring him personally into balance, counteracting his self-absorption. If he could learn to surrender the limelight and risk a true emotional connection, maybe all his interactions would benefit.

The Unhappy One

Most joint readings I do are with couples, so it was interesting to have two close friends come in together. They looked physically similar—same height, same build, same edgy taste in clothes—though one had dark blond hair and the other was brunette. There was even a strong facial resemblance. "People always mistake us for sisters," the blonde said.

The two had met in business school. The blonde founded a marketing firm specializing in holistic and spiritual services, and the brunette, her marketing director, also taught vegan cooking. They'd heard about face reading and were curious. I half-suspected that they wanted to sign me as a client, but they didn't ask.

Instead, they posed a fascinating question. They'd worked side by side and been friends for years, sharing the same experiences, but, as the brunette explained, their temperaments were radically different. "She's always happy. No matter what happens, she sees the bright side. I see only the dark side. Joy isn't a word in my vocabulary. When we succeed at something, she's thrilled, while I fixate on the pitfalls—if the work was hard, what the achievement stopped us from doing, on and on. I'm guess I'm a born pessimist."

"The funny thing is, we look so much alike," the blonde said. "So we're wondering what you can see in our faces that makes us opposites."

Was the brunette actually a born pessimist—predisposed somehow by her personality—or did some aspect of her life make her gloomy? My first impulse was to ask the blonde, "You're the boss and she has to do what you say—does that make her un-happy?" But I bit my tongue.

Looking closely at their faces, I could see the commonalities. They both had strong-boned, muscular jaws, which face readers describe as able to "bite through anything," meaning that both were dynamic and determined. "Your jaws show me that you're productive and that you'll stop at nothing," I told them, which gave them a laugh. But it was true.

Their face shapes were similar enough to suggest they had the same basic interests and values, but there was a clear distinction in their approach to others. For one thing, their hairstyles were very telling. Hair may seem like a fleeting and changeable attribute, but the way you feel comfortable wearing it is a potent expression of personality.

The blonde's hair was parted on the side and fell to about an inch above her shoulders, leaving her entire face visible. When you looked at her, your gaze was immediately drawn to her eyes and forehead. I've mentioned the Chinese expression, "It is written on the forehead," meaning that the forehead is a map of thoughts, whether or not there are perceptible wrinkles. The eyes, of course, are portals of connection, the direct conduit to another person's brain. Having her forehead and eyes fully in view gave the blonde an air of approachability and openness. Even the gap between her hair and her shoulders suggested that she wasn't closed in or self-protective.

The brunette had a high forehead covered by long, asymmetrical bangs, in effect concealing her thoughts. On the left, the bangs swept over her eyelid, hiding most of her eye. Because the left side reflects emotions, that implied that there were feelings, maybe from the past, that she didn't reveal to others or even to herself. The rest of her hair was long and shielding, stretching down her back.

The first focus, looking at the brunette, would be her mouth. Unlike the blonde's mouth, upturned in a relaxed, welcoming

smile, the brunette's was a tense straight line, as if she were pressing her lips together. But the most important feature of her mouth
was the corners. In each corner, there was a pucker, like a dimple.
Face readers interpret these signs as nails or screws, pinning the
mouth shut.

"I see one major difference between you," I told them. "One
of you easily expresses thoughts and feelings, while the other
doesn't or can't."

I turned to the brunette. "Your mouth shows that there are
experiences or emotions that you don't talk about. You just want
to put them out of your mind."

"Wow," she said. "What kinds of things?"

"I can't tell because I don't know enough about your life. One
thing I wonder is whether you have enough freedom."

I asked because she had large, slightly flared nostrils. That's a
sign of needing room to breath, hating constraint, craving space. I
wondered if my initial thought about her employee-boss relationship was correct. At the time, I felt that I was jumping to an easy
conclusion—that the worker would naturally be less happy than
the boss—rather actually intuiting her feelings. This is exactly the
kind of judgment we must suspend in face reading, focusing on
the evidence instead of making assumptions.

"Oh yes," she said. "I love what I do, and I love working for
my friend. We understand and can spark each other creatively. I
have my own teaching sideline, too. I'd say that I have the perfect
degree of freedom."

She had a small nose ring in her right nostril. That clari-
fied my thinking. A piercing implies that the person needs more
grounding in that particular area. In the nostril, especially a large
nostril, it calls attention to the need for freedom. The left side of
the face represents the realm of dreams and emotions, and the

right represents the material world. Hence my surmise that the brunette wanted more autonomy at work or perhaps even to start her own firm.

But since that was not the case, there is another interpretation of the sides of the face. The left side relates to the mother and the right to the father. So I said, "Then I think your unhappiness comes from unresolved sadness in the past. I believe that it relates to needing freedom and grounding in some issue related to your father."

She didn't contradict me or even answer. So often our minds conjure up the worst possible scenario, like abuse, but the issue could have been anything, like failing to fulfill his expectations. But that was for her to contemplate. Her silence suggested that the insight hit home, and I could only hope that, with this push in the right direction, she could find her way to happiness.

The Legacy

A business owner in Luxembourg asked me to meet with his right hand, a woman in her fifties, who seemed depressed. She did look depressed, wearing a shapeless gray pantsuit that hung on her body like a sack. For decades, she'd been the owner's alter ego, helping brainstorm new projects, coddle major customers and suppliers, resolve managerial conflicts, motivate the staff—in effect, being the glue that held the company together.

She did her job well enough, the owner said, but she'd lost her energy and verve. When I repeated those words, her eyes teared up. "That's exactly how I feel."

"What about psychotherapy?" I asked. "That would be ongoing. Face reading is more of a onetime or sometimes thing, not a way to heal."

"I understand," she said. "But maybe face reading can help me pinpoint what's wrong."

Her face showed signs of long-term sadness. Though her lips were generous, the corners of her mouth turned down; and her eyes, even when the tears cleared, looked blurred. Beneath her chin, over the mound of her throat, was an area of swelling, possibly connective tissue weakness, which likely represented a thyroid problem. In Chinese tradition, the thyroid is correlated with the emotions, so thyroid dysfunction leads to emotional problems and vice versa. In German, the expression "having a swollen throat" means being angry. In English the idioms "My heart was in my throat" and "That stuck in my craw" have different shades of meaning but make a similar connection between the throat and feelings.

"Do you have a thyroid condition?" I asked.

She confirmed that she did, so I looked for the source of her troubling emotions. She had classic Bucket face, with a square chin and the sides of her face slanting up to a wide forehead. People with Bucket (or flowerpot-shaped) faces are highly imaginative and multitalented, with the ability to persuade and excite people. They need stimulation to unlock their creativity, so I wondered whether she got that on the job. Being unable to use their talents is often what depresses people.

But she lit up when I asked about her work. "I love it. Every day brings new challenges," she said. "One minute I'm reviewing the blueprints for our new office; the next I'm interviewing prospective heads of personnel; after that, I'll lunch with a customer to discuss a problem, then meet with the staff that afternoon on how to solve it; and I'll end the day with drinks with colleagues or suppliers. It's creative, social, and fun."

"It sounds like your work taps a lot of skills," I said. "That must be satisfying."

"Yes. I've helped build the company from a small firm to a real contender in our field."

To Bucket faces, seeing a vision become something lasting is critically important. Using creative talents is not an end unto itself. They also need a sense that their contribution matters—that it will leave a legacy. Clearly, she had this sense about her work.

So her personal life was the source of the depression. "Do you have a family?" I asked.

"I've been widowed for years," she said. "I do have a daughter and a son-in-law, whom I love."

But she began to cry.

"Is your daughter okay?"

"No," she said, dabbing at her eyes. "Her daughter, just four years old, died of cancer. It's been two years, but she and her husband still suffer so much. It happened so fast—she was sick, and then she was gone. They're just heartbroken."

"What about you?"

"Oh, how I loved my grandchild. I miss her so much. All I can do to fill the void is work."

Her grief was natural, of course, but I immediately saw a dimension to the loss that might be causing her depression. For most people, children are their footprints on the planet, their most tangible legacy. But a visionary would even more intensely view a grandchild as a bridge into the future. With the loss of the child, not just a cherished loved one but also a measure of her vision had died.

"Maybe your daughter will decide to have another child," I said gently, "but what will you do?"

"What can I do? I don't know. How can I ever recover?"

A Bucket face would have trouble finding a path out of darkness. More than other face shapes, they need a trigger to fire their creative thinking, be it a person (like the owner, who'd recognized her abilities), an environment (like the firm, where myriad human and systemic puzzles begged to be solved), or an inspiration (something to strive for on an emotional level, like a cause). Without such a push, a Bucket face doesn't easily find direction.

To heal her heart, she needed something beyond her work—a creative, emotionally satisfying way to make a lasting contribution. If that contribution involved children, so much the better. I got an idea. There was a settlement in her town for refugees fleeing strife in the Middle East, especially the Syrian civil war. My client had mentioned knitting and crocheting among her pastimes.

"Why don't you use your knitting skills to make something for the refugee children? Not necessarily sweaters, which would take a long time, but something smaller?"

"I could make puppets," she said. "I always used to make puppets for my granddaughter."

Within a few months, she sent me a picture of herself at the refugee camp, with a box of hand-knit puppets. Some children were already playing with a few—a unicorn, a mouse, and a dog—so charming, colorful, and clever that you could imagine the pleasure it gave her to make them. Maybe she would have another grandchild, but in the meantime I'm sure that she left lasting footprints on the lives of those refugee children.

The Second Face

In Europe, I was involved with an integrative medicine clinic. One day in the waiting room, I encountered a man in his sixties, who struck up a conversation. He was the facilities manager at a prominent boarding school. It was a very responsible job, managing the upkeep of the building; its systems, like plumbing and electricity; and the school grounds. He even lived in an apartment on the campus.

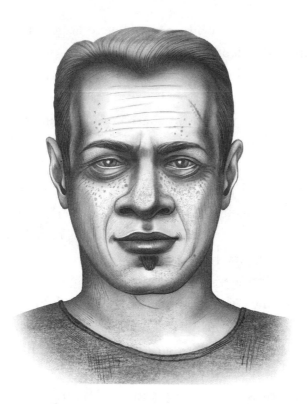

When I asked why he was visiting the clinic, he said, "My eyes. They itch like crazy."

They certainly looked inflamed, with red rims. That can be a symptom of allergies, but the sclera of his eyes and even his skin had a yellowish tinge. The eye inflammation and jaundiced coloring, taken together, strongly implied a massive abuse of alcohol.

Face reading is not about judgment but about getting to the source of the problem. What might be causing or contributing to his drinking?

His hairline formed a widow's peak, a sign of self-determination, as if to say, "I can do things on my own; I don't need anyone else," but also reliability: "You can always depend on me." He had a small triangular beard below his lower lip, which in young men can suggest creativity. But in a man his age, I thought it showed a wish to be in charge, in a position of authority, but not wanting to assert it. His nostrils were large, indicating a love of freedom and independence.

The hairline, beard, and nostrils were sending conflicting messages: wanting to be a leader and a boss yet craving independence from others. He was in charge of managing the school, but his yearning for freedom was worth noting.

I also looked at his hands. Face readers consider a person's hands his "second face" in terms of the information they hold. The section on hands in part III, "A Face-Reading Reference Guide," describes four classic types of hands and their traditional associations. The man had Earth hands, with wide square palms and short thick fingers. That confirmed the reliability I deduced from his widow's peak. People with Earth hands are typically good with their hands, hardworking, organized, and highly pragmatic. I had no doubt that he was skilled at his job.

We look at hands only to support or challenge other observations. The face is our primary source. The man's face was freckled, another sign of longing for freedom. Many of us have freckles when we're young that fade with age. While lots of people retain them in adulthood, they can be hard to detect on a grown man's skin. Known as "stars of the universe" in Chinese tradition, freckles signify a love of travel and far-flung places, the desire to roam the world—an impulse probably thwarted in a man stuck at a school.

The shape of his face was unusual, a combination known as the Deer face. One of its main identifying marks is a pattern of forehead wrinkles: two vertical lines, one on the left and one on the right side of the forehead, like fence posts. The vertical lines don't intersect with the forehead's horizontal wrinkles but, in effect, box them in. Major elements of the Deer face's personality include the need for immersion in nature and the love of serenity.

So I told the man, "The doctor will treat your itching eyes. But I think you know what he'll say about them and your jaundice—that you're drinking yourself to death. You're only in your sixties, a few years from retirement. Why destroy yourself when you're so close to being free to live as you wish?"

He looked stunned but didn't deny drinking. So I went on, "I suspect that one reason you drink is to escape the boredom and confinement of your job."

"That's true," he said. "For the past few years, living on campus has made me stir-crazy. It's required, so I'm trapped. I like my job, but I can never get away from it."

I explained that he had a Deer face. "That means that you belong in nature. You literally need to get out into the woods or to the mountains every day off. You could just hike or you could build something, like a firepit or a stone wall to enclose a clearing, to use your hands creatively and anchor yourself there."

"I feel calmer just thinking about that," he said. "What you're saying makes sense. Studying plants and animals was what I loved most at school. My apartment is full of nature magazines."

"You might also start planning what you'll do when you retire—give yourself something to look forward to."

"I haven't given it much thought. I figured maybe I'd travel."

"Of course, you'll travel," I said, explaining the significance of his freckles. "Nature travel, especially, would be great for you—seeing Yosemite and Yellowstone in America, for example. But what would be absolutely ideal, uniting the tendencies I see in your face, would be for you to lead in nature. You could lead nature hikes or eco tours. You could do it part-time to stay independent and travel whenever you wanted, but also use your take-charge management skills."

"Eco-tour leader—I like that," he said. "I should read up on places that give those tours and start making connections. Maybe there's a training course or something."

"It's worth investigating, to fortify yourself with nature fixes for the next few years and, instead of staying miserable and stuck—and, most damaging, drunk—to begin moving toward the future."

6

Life Purpose

When you meet someone for the first time, the opening question always seems to be, "What do you do?" not, "What do you care about?" or "Who are you?"

In the same way, people often ask, "Why am I unhappy?" or "What's missing in my life?" but miss the core question, "What am I here for?"

We're all put on this earth to fulfill some Life Purpose, which might be defined as "what your personality qualifies you to do" or "what will make the most of who you are."

What your personality prepares you to do depends on many factors, both innate and acquired. Temperament, for example, may be innate. Your face shape and features may offer clues as to whether you're most suited to a structured, predictable environment, with easy-to-meet expectations; prefer to be challenged but need concrete goals; are a self-starter who loves to improvise; thrive when working from the sidelines in management, helping others succeed; or are such a free spirit that you can't bear restrictions at all.

Note that none of these perceivable traits describes what you actually do, yet they describe your essence. The same is true of detectable gifts, like creativity, leadership, passion, dynamism, resilience, rationality, authority, diplomacy, or the capacity to communicate or entertain. These are inborn tendencies that may point to certain professions or other means of fulfillment, but more likely they will help color in the picture of the personality. (A tiny fraction of those I see have an exact niche in the world written on their faces, but usually it takes other clues to zero in on specific talents and directions, as described in chapter 8, "Life Path.")

Identifying such abstract elements of a person's nature is what makes a life-purpose reading so challenging. It involves determining the main forces in an individual's personality, considering how the individual could live that personality in the most winning way, and assessing which gifts the person has to help him or her achieve that goal—active, unused, and even unrecognized talents—as well as fears and other obstructions that might impede progress. The sum of these factors is the client's Life Purpose.

Once I ascertain a person's Life Purpose, I offer him or her two kinds of tools. The first is a group of "life sentences." Life sentences are guiding principles, like a to-do list, that can help organize people's efforts to circle closer to their Life Purpose. I usually tailor about ten maxims to an individual, based on traits I perceive. For example, for someone who talks in a tense, pinched way, one sentence might be, "Learn to give joy to your mouth." For a loner, I might say, "A strong identity can be built together, not alone." For a self-absorbed person, the sentence "Believe in nature as well as people" might help him or her shift focus. I might tell a perfectionist—in the metaphoric style of a Chinese master—"Remember, even the moon has a dark side."

Here are some examples of life sentences that are fairly widely applicable:

- Break free of those who underestimate you.
- Learn to lead with kindness.
- Learn to let go.
- Don't burn out others—or yourself.
- Achieve emotional stability and security.
- Don't step into the fog—be clear on your next step.
- Act with your head and heart together, not separately.
- Don't fear or be influenced by the opinions of others.
- Expect less (or more) of yourself.
- Just exist; don't react to every challenge.
- Get off the carousel of errors.
- Don't just daydream—dream productively.
- The unknown must always be respected.
- Give others space so you have room to breathe.

The second tool is an archetype, an image that represents the Life Purpose. Carl Jung, the philosopher-psychiatrist, believed that archetypes like the Sage, the Wise Old Woman, the Mother Goddess, and the Trickster are shorthand conceptions of human qualities common to every culture. I was taught to use archetypes by Chinese masters, who had their own iconography based on their traditions, so I draw mine from a variety of sources.

There are any number of archetypes to which a person might be assigned, and the art of choosing them could be a book unto itself. When I give a client an archetype, I always interpret what it means, which usually resonates. If two face readers use archetypes to describe the same person, the names might be different, but very likely the interpretations they offer will be almost the same.

The key is to find an image that rather precisely captures what the individual's features reveal.

Some examples of archetypes follow:

- **Guardian Angel of Life:** could apply to a physician, a naturalist—anyone who heals or conserves living things
- **Bridge Builder:** could apply to a diplomat, mediator, or mentor sharing knowledge with the next generation
- **Mother of All:** could apply literally to a maternal figure or to a man who's a protector and nurturer
- **Magician of the Night:** someone who brings light into darkness, who lights the way for people
- **Oracle:** someone who speaks bluntly, with authority, about the future
- **King Priest:** could apply to any visionary leader, from a politician to an inventor/executive like Steve Jobs

I typically choose from a bank of forty or fifty different archetypes, though in some cases I have to look beyond them. Subtle distinctions can make a difference in the client's self-perception. Take my own case, for example. I have a strong Fire face and a very flexible mouth. Fire faces are passionate and impulsive and usually on the move—they hate to stay in one place. A very flexible mouth suggests a potent gift for communication. I had used these qualities in my business career—communications in my work in radio and public relations and travel as a manager. But I had crashed, physically and mentally. I was using my gifts but not coping with the pressure.

When my Chinese master assigned me the archetype of Messenger, I was surprised. "That role didn't work for me at all," I told him. "How could that be my Life Purpose?"

"You interpreted your Life Purpose the wrong way," he said.

"You were living as a Herald. A Herald in ancient times lived in the castle. He'd get his orders from the king, jump on his horse, then ride to the villages, where'd he'd unfurl his scroll and proclaim, 'Hear, hear! The king declares . . .' You liked having the king's favor and being the only trusted Herald, you liked your horse"—I did love my company car—"and you liked the gold coins showered on you for your service. But more and more, you doubted the orders you were passing on. You were putting your heart and soul into products and businesses you didn't believe in. A Herald could do that easily. But not you, because you weren't made to deliver a king's orders. You need to express authentic passion through your own messages. When you can travel the world and speak your own truths, you'll be living your Life Purpose as a Messenger."

That's what I do today. As a Messenger, I feel that I fully inhabit my Life Purpose. But what my Chinese master pointed out is a common dilemma. When you're living in a way that runs counter to your Life Purpose—say, if you are a rooted Tree face working as a traveling salesman—you tend to feel ill at ease and try to change the situation. But when you're living in a way that's close to your Life Purpose—say, as a Herald instead of a Messenger—it can be much harder to recognize that you're on the wrong track.

A final word: before you really embark on discovering or trying to live your Life Purpose, it's advisable to get your life in relative balance. If you're in the throes of a bad divorce, homeless and struggling to survive, coping with a grave illness, or have some other acute, serious preoccupation, your immediate purpose is right in front of you: to get stabilized. Trying to reach for a larger Life Purpose before that happens is like trying to drive a race car with two flat tires.

The Languid Dreamer

As research (and for fun), I often stroll with my friend, a photographer with an old wooden camera, looking for interesting faces. I spotted one at the cheesemongers' stand at the Borough Market in London. What struck me was the discrepancy between selling cheese and what his face suggested: that he was a creative personality. He certainly did not look happy.

Even before I saw his face, his shirt caught my eye. It was buttoned all the way up, to below his chin. It seemed to shout, "I'm uncomfortable. I'm constrained. Set me free!"

He had a sensitive Jade face, which is somewhat unusual for a man, with full lips and a delicate nose. His eyes were like those of Garfield, the cartoon cat, with large pupils and close-fitting, half-

shut lids, which are the mark of an imaginative daydreamer. They also slanted downward at the outer corners, giving him a strong air of dejection and victimization. The archetype that sprung to mind as I looked at him was the Servant.

I wondered if he was compelled to sell cheese because it was the family business or because he needed the income and lacked other focus and direction. Clearly, he was out of balance—dragged down, seemingly trapped in a situation he resented—which made it impossible to ascertain his true Life Purpose.

"May we photograph you?" I asked.

He agreed, and as we chatted I was struck by his air of lethargy. He wasn't lazy or slacking off on the job, but he was mentally stuck, unable to clearly formulate, never mind pursue, the visions in his head. This kind of inertia is an all-too-familiar problem.

Some of us don't fulfill our potential because we're paralyzed with self-doubt; exhausted by supporting others or by making a living; too impatient to learn a craft or to work for long-term, undefined rewards; and so on. But some of us, for whatever reason, just don't muster the energy.

If he'd had an artistic sideline, which would be typical of a Jade face—painting or photography or otherwise creating things of beauty, even making the cheese—he might not have found working at the market so defeating. He mentioned feeling frustrated by the limitations of his job, but he lacked a more fulfilling vision.

"I'm just not sure what else I can do," he told me.

"There's only one way to find out," I said. "You don't have to quit your job, but you need to push in new directions—toward anything that gets your creative juices flowing. What are your ideals? What are your interests? Don't expect to stumble on the perfect answer right away. Keep seeking stimulation. Not only will it shake your lethargy, but eventually you'll find out what you're good at.

Where the mind goes, the energy follows. But first you have to start moving—to make an act of self-will, a conscious effort."

Pinned Ears

One of my clients, a French regional politician, was born with, in his words, "ears like Dumbo." When he was a teenager, thinking he'd be ridiculed, his parents had his ears pinned closer to his head. Now middle-aged, he was convinced that the "pinning" had derailed his Life Purpose, making him a follower instead of the daring leader he longed to be. "What if I get the surgery undone?" he asked. "Could that affect me psychologically?"

The expression "pin his ears back" has two very different meanings. One is to "be on high alert," ready to react; and the

other is, "force him to submit; curtail his actions." He obviously felt that the second definition applied to him. "I haven't felt like myself since I had it done," he said. "It's like I'm inhabiting an alien body."

Those were strong feelings, but as I told him, no one could predict whether freeing his ears would free his mind. Would some inborn authentic self he had until the surgery reemerge? Or would he wake up stuck in the same issues? In Chinese face reading, the ears represent the realm of childhood, so I urged him to consider the emotional backdrop of his upbringing. Did the surgery seem to symbolize his parents' disapproval of the young man he was becoming? Did they find him restless, hard to handle, needing to be reined in? In other words, did he simply look odd to them or did he somehow violate their belief system?

Though I didn't say so, there was a chance that the reversal itself might be enough to make him feel like a different man. But I could assure him of one thing: "If your ears stick out, some will find them appealing—like an interesting, humanizing quirk—and others will think you look goofy and unserious. So you'll find your behavior changing in response to the way you're treated. You'll either enjoy a new kind of attention or have to defend yourself. That's inevitable. Equally inevitable is the fact that a certain percentage of people will be too self-absorbed even to notice a factor as significant as your ears."

He laughed, but I could see that he was carefully weighing my words. Some time later, I got a thank-you card saying that he'd decided to schedule the reversal. "Wish me luck!" he said.

Stars of the Universe

"Bucket face" doesn't sound like a complimentary term, but it connotes good qualities like being stable, down-to-earth, and able

Ears

No two ears are alike—not even the right and left ears on the same person. They are considered an index of a person's ability to process information, as well as his or her drive and decision-making ability. In Chinese face reading, ears tell the story of childhood:

- Ears that stick out indicate restlessness, inability to sit still, too many thoughts in the head.
- Ears close to the head (not visible when looking at the face) indicate being peace loving and seeking harmony and balance.

In Chinese face reading (less so in European), ears are also important indicators of health:

- Bluish ears suggest heart trouble.
- Reddish ears suggest inflammation.
- Deformed ears suggest back pain and disorders of the spine.

Alignment of the ears offers clues about personality:

- Ears that reach higher than the eyebrows indicate impatience and impulsiveness, as well as quick and potentially too-hasty decision making.
- Ears that are roughly even with the eyes or eyebrows indicate a measured approach to life and appropriate speed of decision making.
- Ears that fall below the eyes indicate knowledge seeking, idealism, and perfectionism that may lead to disappointment, and the ability to wait for just the right moment to make decisions.

- Ears that tilt back at an angle, with the lobes pointing forward, indicate a need for recognition and praise, even if unwarranted, and potential selfishness.

The size of the ears is also telling:

- Large, long ears suggest a go-getter personality, a thirst for information, and a high degree of knowledge and life experience.
- Medium-size ears suggest balance and a sense of proportion, selective listening ability, and the tendency to retain what is important.
- Small, short ears suggest sensitivity, fearfulness, and insecurity; shyness and proneness to information overload; and ability to benefit from information.

An odd fact is that older people rarely have small ears. Some believe the reason is that ears grow over time, and others hold that people, as they age, dehydrate and lose mass, so the ears become more prominent.

to inspire others. Other features, especially the mouth and eyes, reveal how those qualities are expressed. Those were the clues showing me that an Asian businesswoman who consulted me fit the archetype of a Pioneer—not a builder, but an explorer.

But at that point, she was fifty-eight. She'd spent her life launching projects, hiring people to execute them, and then moving on to the next challenge. Her career was taxing physically, because it involved travel, and mentally, because she was on a fast-moving treadmill of reinvention, judged not by her accomplishments but by the strength of her next idea.

"Is it time to settle down?" she asked. She had offers of

high-paying 9 to 5 executive jobs that would allow her to put down roots. But the scattering of freckles across her nose, which Chinese face readers call "stars of the universe," strongly implied that she would feel stifled in a conventional role.

Freckles are much debated among face readers. Some Hindu ones, who believe in past lives, or Taoists, who recognize a cycle of transmigration, would say that a person with lots of freckles has collected wisdom over the ages to share with the rest of us. Other Chinese face readers go down the rabbit hole of analyzing what the placement of each freckle means. My own Chinese master advised, "Don't get lost in that. Just look for the most prominent freckles or moles—they tell the story." Certain masters who favor that approach would add that less prominent freckles or moles are mere camouflage, an effort to obscure the personality revealed by the biggest markings.

My client was not covered in freckles but had just a dusting, signifying worldliness, in the sense of "belonging to the world." It meant that she might pause to take a leadership role here and there or put down roots for a while but would never want to stay put. This tendency was confirmed by the shape of her mouth, which was small but with full, highly flexible lips. It was the mouth of a passionate communicator, one who speaks from the heart. Not in the commanding way of a King face, with limited mouth movements, but with the emotional expressiveness to touch and inspire. Her leadership message would be, "Let me show you what I've discovered. It's exciting. Let me take you there."

Her gaze was very steady, highlighting her ability to focus attention closely on a person or on a goal. Her eyes were not wide open and staring but half-lidded, suggesting the daydreams of a visionary. All these elements led me to sum up her personality as a Pioneer, a woman of the world who was drawn to explore, who could integrate her discoveries with her dreams, and who could inspire and guide others to realize them. Then she'd uncover a new passion and dream up a new means for its execution.

At fifty-eight, she was still unearthing new ideas. She wasn't yet ready to take on the yoke of routine. She was meant to be on the move.

The Guardian Angel

A young woman approached me for a reading at an alternative medicine convention. Many clients wonder what to do with their lives, but this woman already knew. "I'm a sales manager for a natural foods company," she told me. "But I've always wanted to help people more directly. I got my undergraduate degree in physiology, with a concentration in complementary medicine, then did the coursework to get certified as a naturopath. That was a few years ago. I keep taking classes and maintaining my certification, but I can't convince myself that it's time to start my own practice."

"Why not?" I asked, though I could see the reason in her face: security. A sales job, dealing with people, would be comfortable enough for a Jade face. She was afraid to leave the regular paycheck and structure of a corporate job to found and run her own business.

As I listened to her explanation, I watched her mouth, which was perfectly balanced, with well-shaped lips. Her words were also measured, suggesting that she knew what she was talking about. But her eyes gave a different message, nervously darting from left to right. Having a mouth and eyes out of sync can mean different things, depending on the context, but the jumpiness often means you're expecting a dramatic change. Since she was talking about a cherished dream, it suggested that she was ready to make it happen.

Was it the right dream? The right time?

She had a classic Jade face, full of passion and love of people. When she smiled, her gums were visible, indicating that she had the belief system of a giver, the desire to help and support others. Most telling, she showed me a new U-shaped line in her face, stretching from beneath her chin up the sides of each cheek. It had no doubt been forming over the years she spent studying toward her degree, getting her certification, and continuing her studies. This is the line of responsibility, the line of the nurturer and care-taker.

"Every element of your face is related to helping and healing," I told her. "Even your hands—sensitive, receptive Water hands—are health-promoting. The archetype I would use to describe you is the Guardian Angel of Life. That is your Life Purpose, as you've known for years. Don't you want to live it?"

"I do," she said. "I just worry that I have so much to lose."

"You mean if you fail? We can fail at anything, whether it's a misguided effort or what we're born to do. No one can decide what's best for you, but I can confirm that you've chosen the right path."

Being a Jade face, she had to guard against timidity and inde-cision. I gave her a list of life sentences to contemplate:

Don't let security limit you.
Resist self-doubt.
Embrace adventure.
Trust your instincts; trust your talent.
Don't trust your head, which will doubt anything.

"I guess that's what I hoped for in this reading," she said. "Validation of my direction, a vote of confidence, maybe a push off the cliff."

The Square Peg

Some of us make or drift into life choices that run counter to our personalities. We may even be very successful. Sometimes a face reader will spot traits, like hidden talents, that explain why this apparent contradiction actually provides a degree of balance. But there are people who continue to feel like square pegs stuck in round holes. That was the case with one of my clients, a Greek woman in her thirties, who was offered a promotion to director of a hotel in Austria. I'd read her once in the past, when she was the hotel's head of human resources, and then again when she was weighing the offer.

When we first met, one of the things that struck me was the squareness of her shoulders, as if she were consciously holding them in place to look bigger or braver. That made her look physically tense. The other feature I immediately noticed was her overdeveloped, muscular jaw—a King-like trait in a face with no other King elements.

There are three reasons why such an out-of-place, muscular jaw would develop in a woman's face. Probably the most common reason is teeth grinding, a sign that the subconscious is actively rebelling against some aspect of daily life. The second is excess testosterone, which can by boosted by intense exercise—that's why many female athletes have it—or by a diet heavy in red meat. The third, of course, is genetics, though it can be hard to tell nature from nurture. If a woman's father has a strong jaw and her mother doesn't, it's worth asking whether she found her mother's role limiting and, perhaps unconsciously, modeled herself on her father.

But apart from her King-like jaw, the hotel director had a pure Jade face, perfectly egg-shaped, with fine features and large, alluring, half-lidded eyes. With her pale skin, dark hair, and sinewy build, she had an appearance that some might consider beautiful and others quite severe. When she smiled, I could see her gums, signifying that she was a giver. Her mouth was wide and welcoming, but she pursed her lips when she spoke, as if spitting out words instead of speaking freely. That suggested that she was holding back, giving of herself unwillingly.

"How did you wind up in the hotel business?" I asked.

"I started out wanting to work in mental health," she said. "But I did a gap year abroad and worked in a psychiatric hospital. It was disillusioning, to say the least. I thought I'd be helping with art and music therapy, but the patients were so drugged up that it was like a babysitting job. When I complained that we weren't actually helping people, everyone made fun of my idealism. Around that time, I met the man who became my husband."

"Are you still married?"

"Oh no," she said. "He worked for a firm that staged events for big corporations. It was the opposite of what I was doing—creating celebrations instead of witnessing human misery. We were acquaintances when he hired me to work in his department, but pretty soon we started dating and got married. After that, no matter what I did, no one took me seriously. I was just the wife of so-and-so, and it hurt our marriage. I left and got a job at the hotel."

"You've been here for a while."

"Yes. But after I quit, my husband started having affairs when he traveled for events. There was so much gossip about it that it got back to me. I was so humiliated that we split up."

I wondered if that was when she started grinding her teeth.

"Here, my work is valued," she told me. "People respect me."

"Is it creative enough?" I asked. "I'm sure you enjoy working with people as head of human resources. But I wonder if part of the appeal is the respect and not being underestimated."

"Maybe," she said. "I felt invisible for so long. And it's been hard to recover my self-respect after the divorce."

When I was back at the hotel a few years later, she badly wanted a reading. "I don't know what to do," she said. "It's a huge honor to be offered the director's job. But I've been so frustrated. The higher up I go in the company, the more administrative my job gets. And the hours—the hotel runs 24-7, so all I do is work. There's no love in my life, and I miss that. As the director, I'll be sacrificing everything—even my chance to have a family—for a goal I don't know if I care about. I mean, running a hotel isn't exactly saving the world."

"I think that's what you're missing as much as love," I said. "The sense of purpose and the satisfaction of helping, even healing, people."

The archetype that described her, at that point, was the Follower—a person who goes where she's led rather than chooses her own direction. That was not who she was meant to be. I reminded her of the qualities of a Jade face—love of beauty, love of people, open-mindedness, and willingness to learn. I pointed out the giving nature suggested by her gums and other factors in her face. "If you feel strongly that you'll be giving up your life for too little, you should think about what would be worth the sacrifice."

"You're right," she told me.

A short time later, she sent me an e-mail. "I turned down the job. I'm going back to school for a degree in psychology, my first love. I might want to work with children and incorporate music and art therapy. What do you think?"

All I could say was, "Brilliant!"

The Mother of All

One day, a young woman dropped by for a nutrition reading. I was expecting a client, so we made an appointment. As she left, I said, "Congratulations on your pregnancy."

"How did you know?" she asked.

The tip-off was that one side of her forehead had splotches of brownish pigmentation called melasma. Also known as chloasma or the "mask of pregnancy," it may be caused by other hormone disruptors, such as birth control pills, thyroid disease, and even stress, but pregnancy is the most common explanation. Melasma may appear elsewhere on the face—the bridge of the nose, the chin, the cheeks, the upper lip—or on the neck and forearms. It's harmless, and when caused by pregnancy tends to fade on its own. Men also get melasma, but 90 percent of cases appear in women.

"That's a good start for a reading," the woman said.

But when melasma appears in an older woman, it's often correlated with an archetype known as the Mother of All. The Mother of All is not a sweet, apple-pie–baking, self-sacrificing stereotype. She's more like Mother Theresa: warmhearted and loving but also tough and strong. She's an authority figure and a force of nature. These qualities define her Life Purpose.

When I was working in Hong Kong at a prominent hotel, I came across such a woman. She was an Australian expat in her late fifties, the wife of a prominent CEO. She had some genuine curiosity about face reading, but mainly she was bored. She'd never worked, and she had a staff to run her household. Her three grown children were married and in far-flung Sydney, London, and San Francisco. "I visit them and my grandkids a few times a year," she said. "I miss them all so much. I'd spend more time with them if they'd let me."

The melasma stretching across her forehead, though notice-able, didn't diminish her attractiveness. She was pleased to hear that and was also gratified by the details I gleaned from her face in the first thirty minutes. "You flatter me; you're so kind," she told me. "You really see me. You know who I am."

I don't flatter people, but I often describe the strengths I see before moving on to the weaknesses. But she preempted me by asking, "Don't you have anything negative to tell me?"

"There are no negatives in a face," I explained. "But everyone has potentially winning and losing qualities. If I describe losing aspects, it's not to criticize or judge but to help bring your life into balance."

"That's what I want to hear," she said. "I want to know what I can improve."

She had an amalgam of shapes known as the Rabbit face. Its characteristics include the visible gums of a giver and the U-shaped line, beginning below the chin and extending up each cheek, that is the mark of the responsible nurturer and caretaker. But it also incorporates King features.

"Your lips, especially, are King-like, with the lower lip fuller than the upper," I said. "You have small pupils like a King, which shows an analytic instead of empathetic bent. I suspect that you have a bit of the King attitude, which is protective but can also seem authoritarian and rigid. It is this whole complex of features that, combined with your melasma, determine your Life Purpose to be the Mother of All."

She was delighted. "The Mother of All—I love that. I'm proud to have that be my Life Purpose. What losing aspects could that have?"

"Well, you might be a bit domineering," I said. "You men-tioned that your children don't always want you there. You might be critical of the way they live or raise their kids—an understandable temptation for the Mother of All. Maybe you need more than just your kids to fill your life."

"Me? Uh-uh," she said, her voice shaking. Her lower lip quivered in outrage. "No. You're wrong."

Evidently, I'd hit a nerve. She got up and walked out.

Later I heard that she'd complained to the spa manager, who defended me, saying, "You wanted the truth. You asked to know what to improve."

"Still, he never should have said that," she insisted.

But the next morning, she came to apologize. "Maybe I overreacted," she said, "but you don't know my family. I love them, and they need me."

"That's how you see it," I told her. "But you said yourself that they limit your visits. Why wouldn't they want your help? Ask yourself honestly, without your King pride and rigidity."

She shrugged, but then said, "So, what's the point of being the Mother of All?"

"Raising your children was training for your Life Purpose. 'Mother of All' doesn't just mean having a family or proclaiming yourself as its matriarch for all time. It means giving to the right people—all kids, even teenagers and young adults—who badly need your maternal energy. Unless you're traveling to see your children and getting entangled in their lives, you're home and bored. You're wasting your gifts and not fulfilling your Life Purpose.

"There's so much social good you could do right here—with homeless kids, maybe; or runaways. You could run an after-school program for children of working parents. You could start an organization of mothers offering support to single moms—think how much they'd appreciate that. Who better to start such a group than the Mother of All? It's a special Life Purpose."

Her eyes were shining, as if I'd inspired her with brilliant ideas. Being a new face reader at the time, I was surprised she didn't think of them herself. They seemed so obvious. But now I understand that, the closer we are to living our Life Purpose—when we're almost there—the harder it can be to see.

7

The World of Expression

The shape of the face and its fixed features, especially the eyes and the mouth, are the outline of the personality, but to color in between the lines, we have to look at the facial expressions. There are forty-three muscles in the face, of which eighteen to twenty are involved in forming expressions. The more muscles you use in making an expression, the more clearly it will communicate your thoughts. Scientists believe that the face may be capable of as many as ten thousand different expressions, of which about three thousand are related to emotion.

By the way, the saying that it takes more muscles to frown than to smile, which probably dates from early in the twentieth century, is probably not true. What is true is that we unconsciously tend to echo the expressions of others we encounter—to smile at those who smile and frown at those who frown. Studies have shown that people told to frown at people smiling and vice versa have to struggle to overcome their instinct to respond in kind.

Smiling not only makes other people smile, it also makes you

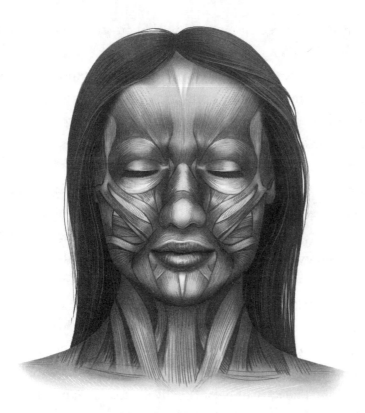

The Muscles of the Face

happier. Smiles, angry frowns, and other facial expressions like fear, sadness, surprise, and disgust, even if faked, can awaken the emotions they depict in us. From Charles Darwin on, many scientists have argued that these basic facial expressions are universal, communicating the same feelings in every culture and even across species. Chimpanzees express the same emotions on their faces as we do.

In 1976 a system was developed, based on the work of a Swedish anatomist Carl-Hermann Hjorstjö, to categorize facial expressions. Known as the Facial Action Coding System (FACS), it defines the expressions and identifies the muscle groups used in creating each one. Psychologist Paul Ekman, a pioneer in the study of facial emotional expression, refined the system, which is not used in interpreting expressions but in studying their under-lying physiology.

Ekman is known for his work with microexpressions, which are tiny, involuntary expressions lasting for a fraction of a second. Because they can't be controlled or hidden, they reveal a person's true emotions. Learning to read microexpressions is one of the greatest challenges for a face reader, but the ability is a very impor-tant tool. In the chapters that follow, I'll often refer to microex-pressions in assessing people's reactions in a given moment, which can offer clues to their deeper nature. For example, a single line between the eyebrows called the hanging needle shows tenacious drive, but the person's microexpressions will show me whether that drive is stubborn unwillingess to compromise or steadfast de-termination. The section "Six Microexpressions" describes how these tiny movements appear.

People often ask me whether Botox and plastic surgery affect face reading. The answer is, not really. Botox is mainly for deleting facial lines, which for an experienced face reader are mostly extra and not primary sources of information. Right after a person gets Botox, the face is frozen, and the muscles barely move, so that's a bad time for a reading. As I've joked with clients, "I can't tell you much about the car because it's parked! Come back when the engine is running."

I warn my clients not to overdo Botox treatments and cos-metic surgery and risk impairing the movements of their facial muscles. Those who go too far may experience a significant dis-ability when it comes to relationships. We connect deeply with others by mirroring their expressions. A person whose expres-sions can't be echoed is hard to bond with and understand, and someone who can't replicate others' expressions will be less able to empathize. Chapter 12, "Perception," discusses the mechanism of mirroring.

Six Microexpressions

Because microexpressions are involuntary, they are a more reliable index of emotion than the same expressions held for a longer period (more than a few seconds). They are universal. Here is the way they appear in every culture:

- *Surprise:* eyebrows raised, skin below the brow stretched, horizontal wrinkles across the forehead, eyelids wide open, jaw dropped without evident tension in the mouth
- *Fear:* eyebrows raised and drawn together in a straight line; forehead wrinkles bunched between the eyebrows; lower eyelids tense and drawn up, but upper eyelid raised; white sclera showing above the iris; lips open and stretched back
- *Disgust:* upper eyelids raised, cheeks and lower lip raised, nose wrinkled
- *Anger:* eyebrows lowered and drawn together, vertical lines between the eyebrows, eyes bulging or staring, lips pressed together, nostrils dilated, lower jaw jutting out
- *Happiness:* corners of the lips drawn back and up, raised cheeks creating a wrinkle from the outer edges of the nose to the outer edges of the lips, and crow's-feet at the eyes
- *Sadness:* inner corners of the eyebrows drawn in and up, jaw drawn up and corners of the mouth turned down, lower lip pouting out

A face reader does sometimes encounter a stone face, one with stiff muscles, because of illness or some personality issue. It is possible, though challenging, to gain a great deal of information from the eyes alone. The opposite of the stone face is the fluid face, which cycles through lots of tiny expressions every minute. It

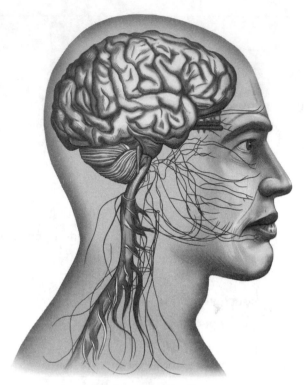

The Nerves of the Face

takes a lot of experience to zero in on the most significant expressions that flicker by, and a lot of empathetic mirroring to interpret them.

Beyond facial expressions, good face readers are attuned to the many other nonverbal cues—body language, gestures, and even clothing styles—that people project. Some of them have tremendous power, as my Chinese master once demonstrated. He'd been invited to talk about face reading at a managers' communications summit. After greeting the three hundred businesspeople gathered in the auditorium, he asked them all to join him in an exercise. "Not you, Eric," he said softly. He took his lower lip between his thumb and index finger, pulled it and began to massage it. After a couple of long minutes, he said, "Now, let's take a break."

"A break?" I said. We hadn't even started.

My master didn't answer. But I was amazed to see that at least a third of the audience got up and headed for the restrooms.

In Traditional Chinese Medicine, parts of the face are related to different internal organs. The lower lip is correlated with the colon.

It was a fascinating lesson, illustrating how a gesture producing a literal effect has the same figurative meaning. A person who is pulling at his or her lower lip is not planning what to do tomorrow but is trying to throw off a problem or eliminate something.

Here is an example of a quick but comprehensive reading drawing on a broad range of cues. I was in a restaurant in Chicago with a friend who wanted a better understanding of what I do. He pointed to a couple seated near us and asked, "What can you tell me about that woman?"

I first noticed that she had a Bucket face, flowerpot-shaped, suggesting that she was creative but possibly had trouble getting started.

Next I looked at her microexpression, which was clearly unhappy—her jaw was raised, her eyebrows were drawn together, and the corners of her mouth turned down. Then she spoke, not articulating fully but talking out of one side of her mouth. That is a classic expression of contempt, not one of the six official primary microexpressions, but very easily understood. "What's wrong with her dinner partner?" I thought. "How did he earn her contempt?"

I was next drawn to her gestures. After placing her water glass on the table, she kept reaching out to check it, to be sure that it

Five Ways of Looking at a Woman

was stable. She did the same with the salt and pepper, even twist-
ing the caps to be sure they were secure. Clearly, that was a sign
of anxiety.

Her body language was also striking. Her shoulders were
sunken and curved forward, as if she were curled in on herself.
Her face was angled downward but when she lifted it, I could see
that her lower eyelids were bluish-violet.

In the space of a minute or two, I had assessed her in five different ways and gleaned enough information to tell my friend, "I
can see that she's stressed out—the stress hormone cortisol and
insomnia cause those blue circles under her eyes—and feels that
life is out of control. She craves support and reassurance. She's not
upset with her companion, or she'd be more erect, confronting
him physically, instead of shrinking into herself. Her contempt is

self-directed—there's something she's longing to do or create, but she can't manage it for some reason."

"Wow," said my friend. "You could see all that?"

Of course I could, and so can we all (or at least most of us). Obviously, the lexicons of gestures and body language are far too vast to attempt listing here, but, as with facial expressions, we're hard-wired to interpret them.

The goal of this book is to make us more conscious of expressions, gestures, and body language in order to awaken our intuitive powers. Many more examples of the intersection of fixed features, expressions, gestures, and body language appear in the coming chapters.

Hanging Tough

If you can't re-create a person's microexpressions, it can be hard to know what they mean. That was an interesting problem that I observed in a client in London, a mild-mannered women who came for a nutrition reading. "I hate walking down your block," she said, "because the guys hanging out on the street scare me."

I hadn't noticed any especially threatening characters, so I asked, "What makes them scary? The way they dress? Their piercings or tattoos?"

"It's their facial expressions. They look dangerous."

"Show me," I said.

She kept trying to twist her face into an expression of menace. She looked so silly that soon we were both laughing.

"Why don't I try?" I said. "Tell me if I've captured it."

I lowered my chin and curled up one corner of my mouth,

staring up at her through narrowed eyes. In my mind I saw myself as a bull getting ready to charge.

"Yes, they look like that," she told me. I encouraged her to try again, but even then her attempt to copy my hostile look wasn't forbidding. By nature, she was nonaggressive, so she couldn't convincingly communicate the feeling.

But even familiar emotions like happiness and sadness are hard to convey credibly if you don't feel them. Sadness, especially, is hard to fake, even if you know that you should raise the inner corners of your eyebrows and pull them together, lift your jaw and pout your lower lip, and turn down the corners of your mouth. Most of us can recognize a phony look of happiness, even if the major elements are present, like a smile that lifts the cheeks and crinkles the corners of the eyes.

One of the biggest clues that a microexpression is real or false is the length of time it lasts. So I asked my client, "How long do those scary looks go on?"

"Those guys scowl at me all the way down the block."

"Then those may not be true expressions of aggression," I said. "A dangerous look, like someone about to attack, will last maybe a second or two. Someone who holds an expression longer than that is making a conscious effort. Those guys may be trying to look tough to impress each other, rather than trying to intimidate you, who pose no threat."

Of course, there's no ironclad guarantee that someone who looks angry is harmless, but as a general rule, an expression that lasts more than five seconds is not authentic. Chapter 12, "Perception," goes into more depth about the Five-Second Rule and the "mirroring" process that helps us intuit the emotions of others.

"That's a relief," my client said. "In unfamiliar places, I do get anxious. I'd better control my own microexpressions so I don't broadcast how nervous I am."

The Embers of Marriage

In Germany I appear on a reality TV show, along with a psychologist and other experts, to help people in relationships. One of the couples on the show was coping with serious illness, the man suffering from colon cancer and the woman from rheumatoid arthritis, chronic inflammation of the joints. Though they'd been together for decades, the husband, then approaching sixty, was almost twenty years older. Now they'd begun to wonder whether their marriage could withstand the dual challenge of illness and aging.

"Do you have children?" was my first question.

"I do," the man said, "from a prior marriage. We moved out of the city to a house in the countryside to make room for them. But now they're adults, raising families of their own."

"The house has gotten impossible to manage," the wife said. "I want us to move to an apartment, but he keeps raising objections. That's the big issue between us."

"That's not our big issue," the man replied. "You won't let me touch you. That's our worst problem."

Everyone on the set—the producers and the technical staff—seemed to freeze at that. I could hear the silence through my earbud.

To break the tension, I asked, "You mean you don't have a sexual relationship?"

"I'm not just talking about sex. I mean no kissing, no hugging, no cuddling—no touching her, period."

"Is that because of pain?" I asked the wife. "Or are you tired of him?"

"It's not about pain or not wanting to be with him. I just don't like the physical contact." The look on her face was not sad or defensive but resigned.

"Were you ever passionate with each other?"

"Oh yes," she said. "Our early years were amazing. Though we were jammed into a one-bedroom apartment, with our two dogs and his young kids, we were always on fire! We couldn't keep our hands off each other. But now, with big empty rooms and all the privacy we could ever want, we don't connect that way anymore."

"What kind of relationship do you have then?" I asked. "Would you call it love?"

"Definitely," the man said. He listed the elements of a loving relationship—mutual attraction, physical and mental compatibility, shared life goals, making the other person happy, sympathizing with the other's pain, and more. He wound up by saying, "Our marriage may be missing some of these aspects right now. But since I love her, I'd call our relationship loving."

"What would you say?" I asked the wife.

"I wouldn't exactly call it loving. I'd say that our relationship serves a purpose. We need and look after each other."

In my earbud, I could hear reactions from people on the set. While the husband spoke, they were approving, touched by his loyalty and tolerance. Now there were murmurs about the poor guy loving her when she just wanted a caretaker, about her not deserving him, and so on.

As a face reader, I don't take sides, and I don't base my evaluations on words. Instead, I studied their faces to assess the situation. The husband was a classic Mountain face, with a backward-sloping forehead narrower than his jowls. Mountain faces are typically loners, though they're capable of great loyalty. They communicate well, as the husband had in defining love, but they tend to repress feelings and withhold emotions. They can also be chronic procrastinators, waiting out problems in hopes that they'll disappear rather than addressing them.

Surprisingly, the wife had a pure Fire face—triangular, with a pointed chin—which is associated with vibrancy, passion, and love. When living in a winning way, a Fire face is self-assured and strongly supportive of others, but when living in a losing way, can be plagued with self-doubt. The wife's rationality and lack of ardor didn't add up. Where was the vivid emotionality I would have expected? I could detect only fleeting glimpses.

So I told her, "Your face contradicts the detachment in your words. I see that you're passionate, even impulsive by nature. Your microexpressions reveal anger and frustration—your eyebrows are drawn together, your lips are pressed shut, you pinch the bridge of your nose—but I don't see signs of resentment toward your husband, like a corner of your mouth curled up in contempt. So I think you're frustrated and angry with yourself."

She immediately began to cry great, soaking tears. When she could catch her breath, she said, "Yes. I'm furious that I just can't function. My joints don't work and my body's stiff, like a robot's. I'm too young to feel a hundred years old. Since there's no cure for rheumatoid arthritis, I'll probably get worse, with even more pain and limitation. I'm not myself now, and I never will be again."

As she wept, her husband sat there watching, without a word. He didn't make a move to comfort her. He had a deer-in-the-headlights look, as if he could cope only when his wife was lively and confident. Maybe he'd seen her despair before and hadn't known how to react. Rather than engage, he'd probably withdrawn. Being forced to confront her vulnerability and anguish unnerved him.

Now the background talk shifted radically: "Wow, all that talk about love, the guy didn't lift a finger, the poor wife . . ."

Of course I didn't judge or criticize the husband. He was such a typical Mountain face. Instead, I said, "You love your wife, and to you that means making her happy and sympathizing with her pain."

"Yes, that's right."

"So why don't you hear her need to move somewhere easier to manage?"

"Well, I do hear it. I'm not saying we can't do it, but there are so many decisions to make. First of all, to unload our current place, we'd have to varnish the floors and put up new wallpaper. Then, we'd have to find a place without stairs. We'd be cramped in an apartment, with no outdoor space . . ."

The list went on and on. A Mountain face often resists major moves. At a certain point, I had to break in before the sheer number of variables overwhelmed him. "You're both sick," I told him. "Maybe a change—a new place—is exactly what you need to heal. It will be a clean slate, a blank sheet of paper on which you can write a new life story. Staying where you are maintains the same thinking patterns, including your illness mind-set. Moving could be a turning point."

His wife had begun smiling as I spoke to him.

"It could especially be a turning point for your relationship. The two of you will have to work hand in hand to choose a new place and get established. In the process, you'll have a chance to rediscover each other, to rebuild trust and possibly rekindle your attraction. You'll be on a fresh footing, starting a new life together."

"Ah, well, okay," he said. "I guess that's worth considering."

Clearly, he was stalling. "The time for considering is past," I said. "You've been mulling this over for a while. I think your wife deserves to know now, 'Yes, I'll move with you,' or else, 'No, I just can't do that.'"

For a long moment he was silent. Finally, he told his wife, "Okay, I promise that I'll try to move."

"Promise to try? That's just a half promise," I pointed out.

Again, he shut down, staring at the floor while his wife kept urging him with her eyes. Though struggling, he ultimately couldn't bring himself to say more than "I promise to try."

But the mood had lightened. Apparently, to the wife, it seemed like progress to have a half commitment instead of a litany of objections. The hidden emotion unlocked from her micro-expressions had started to touch him. We'd begun to move the Mountain.

The Job Interview

Corporations often ask me to evaluate potential hires, especially for major positions. I have a routine that lets me size up the person ahead of time, based on gestures and expressions. I make a point of meeting the applicant in the lobby, loaded down with papers, notebooks, and a laptop. As we enter the elevator, I say, "My hands are full. Would you mind pushing the button for our floor?"

The way the person does it can be telling. Most people press the button with an index finger, which doesn't offer much information. But using the thumb, the most powerful finger, is the sign of a dominant personality, someone who likes to get things done. Pressing the button repeatedly indicates tension.

Using the knuckle or the little finger implies timidity. It suggests a fear of germs, even more strongly if someone with free hands hits the button with an elbow. Those who are afraid of bacteria are likely fearful in other realms of life or, at the very least, out of balance. The people who press the button with the middle or ring finger are individualists, who see the world their own way.

The man a Swiss corporation asked me to evaluate used his index finger, so I got little advance intelligence. Meeting the head of human resources was a final step, I gathered, in what had been a series of interviews. In the director's office, the applicant's résumé and other documents were spread out on the desk. I took a seat beside him to observe as he and the director chatted.

The director was especially keen on some of the applicant's international coursework. "Your background is terrific," he said. "I know that these programs are rigorous, so completing them is a real achievement."

"Yes, they were tough but rewarding," the applicant said. He seemed smooth and confident as they discussed various courses, and the director grew increasingly eager to hear more. "Who was on the faculty then?" he asked. "Did you ever study with Dr. So-and-So? What was the reaction to his book?" and so on.

As the questions grew more and more specific, the applicant managed to keep his composure. But he began to run his thumb and forefinger down the sides of his nose, pinching and releasing his nostrils. This was a tacit cry for help: "Give me space. I can't breathe. I need air." It was the gesture of a man backed into a corner.

Before I could study him more closely, the director's secretary knocked on the door. As the two exchanged a few words, the applicant excused himself to use the restroom. "Something's fishy here," I told the director.

"Do you think so? He seems to know what he's talking about."

"You haven't really looked him in the eye," I said. "You've been swept up in the conversation. So, when he comes back, keep asking those questions, but now stare straight at him."

When the man returned, the director started in again, saying, "I'm so intrigued by your experience. Let me ask you about . . ."

Under scrutiny, the applicant began to lose his cool. He squirmed in his seat and answered in halting, fragmented sentences. He kept pulling at his nose. Now the director, too, could see that he was floundering. Maybe the applicant hadn't exaggerated his credentials, but something was definitely off. His mounting discomfort and lack of candor were troubling.

Ultimately, the company hired another candidate. Our interview wasn't the only reason, but it was an important factor. While it's possible to control our expressions to some degree, most of us are less effective liars than we might imagine.

The Traitor

Corporate clients, especially in Asia, often ask, "What does the year ahead hold? What can I do to make it more successful?" The answer for all of us is to live as authentically—in a way as true to our personalities—as we can.

When I know clients are interested in traditions, as well as contemporary face-reading styles, I sometimes incorporate the old-school maps and charts compiled over the ages by Chinese scholars. One of them is a perpetual calendar of the influences governing each year, which affect people differently based on their personal characteristics. For example, certain years are associated with farewells, either saying good-bye to or being left behind by some person or element of life; others relate to health, which, depending on the person's condition, can mean either recovering from illness or struggling against it. Interpreting how the calendar's symbols for the year—or even any given month—apply to a person requires special training that is beyond the normal scope of face reading.

Such analyses can seem like fortune-telling, which is why I offer them just to clients who value ancestral lore. The credibility of face reading as an art and science has been hard won. But, as the story of one of my clients shows, skilled interpretations of the calendar's symbols can be a helpful backdrop to what faces reveal.

My client, one of the founding partners of an investment firm, had become its CEO. When I was invited to their corporate retreat one November, I was initially struck by how enthusiastic and committed the partners seemed. Talking about a big project, they all had the same expression, with eyes fixed on each other, fully engaged, except for one guy, whose glance would drop and then shift from side to side. That wasn't necessarily a bad sign. It suggested a difference in vision that could just as easily benefit as harm a management team. Still, seeing one partner out of step with the others, I made a mental note to watch him.

Out of curiosity—and because I knew it would appeal to my client—I also consulted the calendar of influences.

The symbology yielded a warning: "The emperor will be betrayed by a general early next year."

When I told the CEO, he was skeptical.

"I can't believe it," he told me. "I trust my partners. We're not the typical cutthroat corporation. We started this company together, so it belongs to all of us. Maybe you're misreading the signs."

"Maybe," I said. "But take it as a word of caution. It can't hurt to keep your eyes open."

A few months later, he called me. "You were right! It's happening. One of the partners is leaving and trying to steal major clients."

"Was it—" I named the man with the dropped and shifting eyes.

"Yes," he said. "How did you know?"

I gave him a few examples of suspicious microexpressions, including the shifting gaze I first observed and another moment when the man did a presentation at a whiteboard, his mouth addressing his listeners but his eyes never connecting. Then I texted the CEO a photo I'd snapped of the founders. The CEO was sitting at the center with the others standing around him. All were facing forward and openly smiling, except for the guy in question, who hung behind them. One of his eyes was trained on the camera, while the other was visibly scanning the room.

Of course, these weren't definitive signs that he was plotting something, but clearly, throughout the retreat, the guy was mentally absent. With the wisdom of hindsight, the evidence looked damning.

"What should I do?" the CEO asked.

Having done a full reading, I'd identified the CEO as a visionary and a catalyst, someone who made things happen. More strategist than client handler, he could still mobilize the troops. So I told him, "You'll be wounded if you fight this battle alone. Pull together the partners and mount a joint defense to keep the clients he's trying to steal."

He took my advice and, with the help of the others, managed to retain most of the major accounts. The betrayer did woo enough to launch his own firm, which got off to a slow start. Microexpressions present the greatest challenge to those studying face reading because they are so changeable. Hard as they can be to interpret, they hold tremendous power.

8

Life Path

In chapter 6, I talked about the importance of recognizing your Life Purpose, the kinds of pursuits that maximize the potential of your innate personality. But beyond purpose, we also have talents that we're destined or meant to use, for both pleasure and fulfillment. Those who can dedicate a significant percentage of time to pursuing their talents, or who have the chance to use most of their multiplicity of talents, tend to be the most satisfied and happiest.

In face reading, we call the talents we're born with our "destiny," though I'm using the word cautiously here because of its association with fortune-telling. "Destiny," for our purposes, means observable potential, which is often detected not just from our fixed features but also from clues like facial expressions and gestures (as discussed in chapter 7) and acquired features like certain facial lines.

A few examples of talents that can be seen in the face include the following:

- The talent for communication—a wide mouth with full lips connotes many things, from extroversion to an intuitive bent, which may also include a talent for inspiring others, for entertaining, and for self-expression. A flexible mouth is able to craft messages and convey them to others, which might be helpful in fields like journalism, advertising, and public relations.
- The talent for numbers—a grid of lines on the forehead signifies this talent, which may or may not indicate skill in mathematics. It can also mean being skilled in any methodical, structured pursuit.
- The talent for observation—wide eyes with big pupils connote qualities like dreaminess and creativity. But they also imply an ability to spot details others might miss and quickly assess situations, to predict how they'll turn out.

Many of us don't have the chance to express our talents in our work. But it is possible to achieve your destiny—that is, to use your inborn talents—outside your career, as the stories in this chapter show.

The Butcher's Blues

A man in his sixties came to see me at the urging of his wife, who'd attended one of my lectures. "She thinks maybe you can help me," he said. "I'm just so depressed. I've been seeing psychotherapists for five years, but it's not really helping."

"What's your life situation?" I asked. While depression has many possible sources, face readers traditionally attribute it to unused talents. Since our inborn talents define our Life Purpose, keeping them locked inside inevitably leaves us frustrated and unfulfilled.

He was a butcher, famous in his region of France for his artisanal sausages. "I have a great business," he told me, "with branch stores headed by my two terrific sons. I'm still crazy about my wife, and I love our beautiful home. I have no reason to feel so blue, but I can't shake it."

As he spoke, I glanced at his hands to see if they contradicted my initial impression of his face. A clear mismatch, which we sometimes see, would offer clues about the cause of a depression related to unused talents. But in his case, the hands and face were relatively in sync. The butcher had Earth hands, which are short and square, with thick fingers the same height as the palm. They were the hands of a craftsman, one gifted at working with them, surely a necessity in his profession. People with Earth hands also tend to be honest, pragmatic, well-organized, hardworking, and ambitious, if perhaps a bit insensitive and unimaginative. But, for me, hands are just a backup, so I studied his face for more reliable information.

His face was fleshy but with a nose smaller than you'd expect, reinforcing the practical work ethic his hands suggested. No wonder he was successful in business. His mouth was a bit wider than average, with full, very shapely lips. That was a sign of creativity, which he probably expressed by adding the herbs and spices that made his sausage famous. So far, he seemed to be using his talents well.

But his eyes and his demeanor told a different story. He had the long eyelashes, large eyes, and big pupils that connote softness, compassion, and imagination. His microexpressions were never abrupt or demanding. Instead, the muscles in his face moved in concert, like a calm wave. Even his speech was warm and colorful, not the crisp and efficient tones of a businessman. "How did you become a butcher?" I had to ask.

"Well, my father was a butcher," he told me. "I was raised

in the shop, and when I inherited it, I gave it more of a gourmet spin. I seemed to have a knack for the business."

"That makes sense," I said. "But I think it troubled you to kill animals."

"Oh yes, always. I've never gotten used to it. But I'm a butcher's son, and I know that someone has to do it. I try to be merciful about it."

"That's one element of your depression," I told him. "But I think another is that what you make is impermanent. You put your heart and soul into producing great, delicious sausages that give pleasure for a moment but then vanish."

I couldn't see his destiny, of course, but only signposts suggesting its direction. "The key for you may be using the gift of working with your hands to create something beautiful and enduring." In my mind was the image of a sculptor, chiseling an image out of stone. He listened attentively and thanked me.

Some time later, I got an email saying that, at last, his depression had lifted. It was a trip to Sicily that changed him.

While exploring Catania with his wife, they happened upon a ceramics workshop, where he was enthralled by the potter's wheel. He asked to try it, and, as if by instinct, his hands knew how to handle and shape the clay. Thrilled to discover his talent, he began to study pottery back in France. Within a year, he'd turned the butcher shops over to his sons. He opened his own pottery studio, where he could sit in the courtyard, with the sun on his face, making crockery to sell to the tourists.

"I'm so happy now," he wrote. "Your words about creating enduring beauty touched me deeply. They inspired me to look for ways to do it. And now, late in life, I've finally found where my heart lies."

The Stressed Dentist

In Bangkok, I met a celebrity dentist—highly successful, with a glittering clientele—who suffered from headaches and mood swings. At first, I suspected a nutritional problem, likely a need for magnesium, given his jumpiness. But I detected no evidence of deficiency. Seemingly well nourished, he was also well groomed and well dressed—apparently well off in every way.

Scanning his face, I was surprised to see that he lacked the gift of healing or even a talent for working with his hands. "Do you like your work?" I had to ask.

"Well, as jobs go, it's not bad," he told me. "Not only do I have a very comfortable life, it's given me accomplished and fascinating friends—a real niche in society."

I could see why his practice flourished. He had a Moon face, round and full, with the "mouth of the moon," which is wide and welcoming but with very thin lips. These are the features of an entertainer—the mouth especially. An entertainer who loves to amuse or ply people with pleasantries, rather than dwell on feelings and emotional connections. I could imagine him putting his patients at ease with jokes and happy chatter.

But his eyes were small, with very small pupils, implying a more analytic nature than a healer's empathy. When he laughed, he showed no sign of gums, which suggested that he wasn't much of a giver. In those who care for others, there is often a U-shaped "line of responsibility," which begins under the chin and stretches up the cheeks. It means, "I'm so concerned with others' needs that I often forget myself." He had no evidence of that line.

The dentist's hands reinforced my impression of his lack of healing talent. They had large square palms with deep lines and long, thin fingers. These are Air hands. People with Air hands are usually live wires: vibrant, fast-living, and easily bored. They love to communicate, often with animated gestures, but are more logical than emotional. Typically, they're more interested in knowledge than in other people.

"I think you became a dentist through sheer will," I told him. "You have a strong intellect, and I'd say that what you find most stimulating about your work is problem solving."

He agreed, admitting that his family had pressured him to enter a lucrative profession. It did give him pleasure to make money.

It showed in his face. He was in his forties, so his face was relatively smooth, but his forehead's horizontal lines were crosshatched by a faint but distinct vertical set. The lines formed a grid, which is a characteristic sign of mathematic talent. People with such crosshatching, especially when combined with analytic small eyes and pupils, tend to become bankers, stockbrokers, or financial advisers.

So he was a social butterfly and a numbers guy. What did that add up to? Suddenly, I got a stroke of insight. "I bet you love to gamble."

"Yes, I do!" he said. "At least once a month, I go to Macau and hit the tables—cards, craps, roulette, you name it. I win a lot, since I have systems, but even when I lose, I'm in my element. So, should I become a professional gambler?"

"Definitely not," I told him. "You enjoy it too much to stay disciplined. Maybe you need a dual focus, using your entertainment gift to develop a circle of numbers-minded friends—people to gamble with or to pursue some other mathematical interest. That could boost your moods by giving you something to look forward to when you get fed up, bored, and frustrated with your work. It might help your headaches, too."

"Hmmm," he said. "That could be fun. Maybe I should start an investment club . . . I'll keep thinking."

The Music Man

At a party, a man in an expensive-looking business suit introduced himself and shook my hand. His fingers were so long and thin that, were it not for his conservative attire, I would have pegged him as a piano player. His perfect grooming—a very close shave and carefully styled hair—reinforced his top-executive image. Still, up close, he had artistic features—very full lips and the half-lidded eyes of a dreamer. His face was a combination Jade, suggesting creativity, and Moon, the shape of an entertainer.

But the most intriguing clue was the shape of his ears, which you might call the ears of attunement. Many musicians have these

ears, which may also indicate a kind of sixth sense, a heightened sensitivity to other people and their surroundings.

His ears were small and filmed with fine, silvery, almost invisible hair, like the peach fuzz you see on babies. Most of us lose ours in childhood, but quite a few retain vestiges, as he did. The hair was inside and outside the ear and even on his earlobes, which were attached directly to the jaw, without drooping. The absence of space between the lobes and the jaw is another sign of sensitivity and, possibly, mood swings.

As we chatted, I asked, "What do you do?"

"I run a hedge fund," he said. You'd expect a hedge fund manager to have features like a secretive mouth and the cross-hatched forehead of a math whiz. Instead, his forehead had only two lines, a deep, prominent material line and, above it, a strong ego line. Above his right eye, there was a line signifying instinct, but not above the left, which would show intuition. As I tell clients, the instinct line is about you, and the intuition line deals with others. Good instincts could help him in finance, but lack of intuition might hurt relationships and, at worst, make him very selfish. Of course, that might be a plus for a hedge fund manager.

I must have unconsciously smirked a little at the thought, because he said, "What's funny about that?"

I apologized, explaining that I was a face reader. He was fascinated. "I'll tell you everything I've observed about you," I said. "But would you indulge me by wrinkling your forehead?"

When he did, I could see, right up at his hairline, wispy, disconnected fragments of a third line, the line of idealism, spirituality, and creativity. They implied that he was working to develop a higher consciousness. His deep material line, the lowest on the forehead, indicated a powerful connection to the things of the world, including money. His ego line, in the middle, though less prominent, suggested a strong identity and sense of what he wanted. Those splinters at the hairline might mean that he was performing acts of charity, going to church now and then, reading spiritual books, or possibly, given the other signs I'd noted, beginning to create art.

"I am!" he confirmed, when I presented my findings. "I'm doing a lot of composing these days. I make my living in finance, but I have a whole recording studio in my home, where I play my instruments and work on music. You got it right. Music is my true passion."

9

Business

This chapter might be called "Life Path: Part 2" because it draws heavily on assessments of talents as they're used (or overlooked) in organizations. The "Life Path" chapter focused on the personal fulfillment individuals were able to achieve by using their gifts. But in the corporate world, where I so often consult, the issue is problem solving. It involves a different kind of face reading, looking less into deep questions like Life Purpose and more into interactions and responses to situations. I usually don't have time to—and nor do I need to—sit down with people for an hour and a half to determine what they're all about. Instead, I often read them as they go about their business.

In this more specialized kind of face reading, gestures and facial expressions, especially involuntary microexpressions, play a critical role. While this kind of reading might seem more superficial, it's no less complex because of the timing, the number of people to assess, and the kinds of problems involved.

The Bridge

Steve Jobs famously said, "It doesn't make sense to hire smart people and then tell them what to do. We hire smart people so they can tell us what to do."

But knowing when to apply that wisdom can be a challenge for CEOs, including a client who led a major Austrian textile firm. "We're not hitting our targets," he told me. "Productivity is down. Maybe you can give me some insight as to why."

"Who do you want me to look at?" I asked. "Department heads?"

"Maybe. It might make sense to start with—" He named the person, who turned out to play an unusual role as a liaison between divisions.

The man had a Moon face, typically correlated with great communication skills. Moon faces tend to be loyal and reluctant to lead, so the CEO could count on him to relay orders. Congenial by nature, Moon faces are often diplomatic and able to unite others—all in all, fine qualities for a liaison.

The shape of the liaison's ears implied that his diplomatic acumen was strong even for a Moon face. Instead of being rounded, the outer cartilage was more triangular, slightly pointed toward the back of the head. I suspect that the pointed ears of *Star Trek*'s Mr. Spock were an unconscious adaptation of this shape, exaggerated to seem otherworldly and to stress the style of expression that we associate with Spock: impartial, tactful, and emotionally detached.

The liaison also had lots of lines on his forehead, indicating both that he was constantly thinking and that his interests were so broad as to make him highly receptive to others. A number of the lines were broken, suggesting lack of follow-through on his ideas. As I observed him with different managers, they all seemed to like and respect him. Most of his job involved delivering decrees from the boss, rather than solving problems.

Still, in his interdepartmental role, he was uniquely positioned to see employees' challenges and formulate solutions. "Certain groups here, like sales and marketing, don't sync up well," he told me. "Though I suggest ways to coordinate their efforts, they don't really listen. I don't have the authority to push them."

Later, when I conveyed this to the CEO, he said, "So, he has ideas—why don't people act on them?"

"Have you heard his ideas?" I had to ask. "The guy is a great asset—good at collecting information and strategizing. But do you listen to his recommendations? Do you tell managers to act on them?"

"Why wouldn't I listen to him?"

"Because you don't take him seriously," I said. "You're a King face, an aggressive, decisive leader. You manage from the top down, using your liaison to issue directives, rather than benefit from his ability to win employees' trust and help solve their problems. He comes in here, all friendly and full of suggestions, and you dismiss them—nicely, so you don't hurt his feelings. As a Moon face, he's not forceful enough to command your attention."

"That's interesting. . . ."

"Meanwhile, you know that there are problems. You keep telling yourself, 'We need fresh ideas.' But a guy can have fresh ideas and not know how to execute them. That's your strength as a King face, turning strategy into action. To do that, you should listen to the Moon face, the diplomat, who has relationships with employees that you, being the boss, don't have."

"So you think I'm wasting his input."

"It seems like it." It was exactly the mistake Steve Jobs warned against—hiring a smart person and telling him what to do, rather than the other way around.

"You hired the right person," I told the CEO. "Not another King face, with skills like yours, but a guy who's the opposite. Your instinct was right on target."

"That's a relief," the CEO said, with a laugh. "I see now that it's my King face job to take advantage of it."

The Right Hand

A client who'd founded a Balkan tech company was having trouble hiring a new executive assistant. He needed someone to do the administrative work who also had enough digital savvy to deal with corporate clients. I was surprised that the decision was so hard. Since the job paid well, I thought he'd have his pick of applicants. But his previous assistant had joined the company when it was new, and now, years later, having to interview strangers, he felt lost.

When I met him in his office, he'd winnowed down the résumés to two small stacks. "Here are the ones we're going to interview," he told me. "Pile A are my top choices, and pile B are the backups. Will you look through them and see who strikes you as great?"

He was asking not because I know the tech world—I don't—but because, in some European countries, people put photos on their résumés. He was hoping that I'd identify the best candidates by looking at their faces.

There were only three or four prospects in pile A, his first choices, and maybe seven or eight in pile B. Flipping through the stacks, I noticed that the first-choice candidates were older than the backups. "Are these the most skilled?" I asked.

"No, they're all highly qualified."

On closer examination, I observed that most of the backups had a certain look: very expressive eyes and a wide mouth, with full, prominent lips. "These are the communicative ones," I said. "They'd be personable and probably good at charming clients. Don't you want that?"

"Maybe . . ." he said.

We headed off to dinner, planning to start interviewing in the morning. His wife met us at the restaurant. She was a Fire face, very quick and animated. She had the odd habit of putting her hands in front of her mouth when she addressed me, and she never looked me in the eye. Several times during dinner, she fluffed up her hair with her hands, as if she were trying to make herself seem bigger. Since Fire faces can be plagued with insecurity, I suspected that she felt self-conscious. Maybe it made her nervous to meet a face reader, who might interpret her expressions.

I wondered how she and her husband got along. He wasn't the typical King face business leader, but a Jade face, a creative type and lover of peace and harmony. Jade faces can be indecisive, which was probably why he needed help choosing an assistant. They also tend to fear criticism, shrink from conflict, and compromise too willingly.

When we finished dinner, the wife excused herself so we could finish talking over whiskeys. "I think I see your hiring problem," I said. "You're afraid of your wife's potential jealousy. So you're second-guessing yourself, picking applicants who seem the least threatening instead of the ones most suited to your needs. You obviously weeded out the most attractive ones."

"You hit it right on the nose," he admitted. "The older ones are good, but younger people are so much more attuned to tech. They grew up with electronics and, better yet, are up on the latest trends. So I've been agonizing over the decision."

"What would you like me to do?" I asked. "I can watch the interviews and pick the best of the older ones. I can help you choose a younger one, so your wife could blame me. But I have a better idea that might make everyone happy."

"Tell me," he said.

"We'll see all the candidates and select the best four. Then you ask your wife to meet those four with you and help make the final choice."

"What if she hates them all?"

"That would be a problem. But it's worth a try."

A few days later, he called me to say, "You won't believe what happened. She liked two of the younger ones so much that she said, 'You choose.' So I did. I now have a new assistant."

"Congratulations."

"I misjudged my wife," he told me. "I expected her to be impatient and disapproving when I asked for help, but she was actually glad. She loved being involved. So I got both a boost in marital goodwill and the assistant I wanted."

There's a lesson in that for us all: not to be fearful, reflexively expecting the worst from our loved ones. No matter how well or for how long we know them, people can always surprise us.

The Vampire

Some prominent business leaders recognize that their own personalities may affect their companies' success. That's why the new CEO of a Kuala Lumpur import-export firm hired me as his confidential coach. For a week, I shadowed him to help him maximize his ability to inspire and motivate his staff. He called a meeting of the firm's top managers to kick off our evaluation process.

The language of the meeting was Malay, which I don't speak, but words aren't the focus of a face reader. As my client addressed his twelve executives—nine men and three women—I scanned his face, looking first for signs of authenticity. He came across as genuine and enthusiastic. But while he was speaking, out of the corner of my eye, I glimpsed hands reaching across the table for the pastry tray.

There's a reason why sweet refreshments are often served at such meetings. People feel on the spot, fearful of having to perform at a moment's notice, and so instinctively want to bolster their energy. Or, if a meeting drags on forever, people will eat out of boredom. Interestingly, it's almost always the underlings, not the boss, grabbing for the sweets. The boss doesn't need sugar because the listeners' attention stokes his or her energy.

But in this case, his executives weren't just snacking. They were wolfing down the mini Danishes and doughnuts and chugging coffee as if they'd been starving for a week. When it came time for them to speak, they kept their gaze fixed on their reports, never making eye contact with each other or the boss. There was a paralyzed fear in the air, but not the cowering fear of those expecting to be harshly criticized or fired.

Finally, it was break time. In the hallway, my client pulled me aside to ask, "What did you make of that?"

"I think you intimidate the staff," I told him. "Not because you're a tyrant but because they admire you. They think you're a superstar, so they fear displeasing you or even trying to engage with you one-on-one. Their focus on you is intense, which takes enormous energy."

I mentioned the way they'd fallen on the sweets like a swarm of locusts. He'd barely noticed, being engrossed in his presentation.

"They crave sugar to fuel that intense attention. You're an energy vampire, sucking them dry. When they speak, they cringe not for fear of your reaction but because they don't have the strength to connect with you. They're trying to hoard what little energy they have left."

"You saw all that without speaking our language?" he said. "Was it that obvious?"

"I could see and feel it," I told him. This was not the same situation as in "The De-Energizer" story in chapter 5, in which the yoga teacher stole the students' energy to feed his ego. Instead, without his knowledge, the impressive boss magnetically attracted his executives' energy, and he hadn't learned how to replenish it.

"What should I do?" he said. "I don't want to drain or frighten people. I'm trying to build a team."

The first step was fairly simple. "You can use gestures to give energy back to them."

I showed him how he'd been sitting, with his hands clasped in front of him. It was a dignified pose but one that made him a closed system, implying, "I'm giving out nothing. I'm absorbing your input."

"Sitting that way, you consume people. Their intense focus seems to be hitting a wall. But if you simply open your hands when you speak, spreading your fingers slightly and revealing your palms, you'll start to lift their subconscious burden. They'll feel that you're welcoming them and speaking from the heart. In the beginning it might feel fake or unnatural, but keep practicing. Even if you just lift your wrists and forearms off the table, it will make a difference."

He held out his hands and began to flex them open and closed.

"Once you've mastered that, try a bigger gesture now and then. As a conscious act of goodwill, share energy by making yourself seem less imposing. Open your arms a little wider as you say, 'Let's brainstorm about this problem. I know you're all good managers, so I want to hear your thoughts, even if they seem silly. No idea is too offbeat to mention.'"

"Could it really be that easy to get people on board?"

"Isn't it worth a try?" I said. "Depleted, timid managers are ghosts. They contribute nothing."

He agreed. I'm happy to say that, even in the brief time I was there, he made progress toward reinvigorating his team.

The Working Mother

A Danish woman who came to my office had perhaps the most likable demeanor I've ever seen. She wore her long blond hair in a thick, tousled braid dangling in front of her left shoulder. Her eyes crinkled at the corners when she smiled, exposing her gums—the sign of a giving nature. She had several U-shaped wrinkles starting under her chin and rising up each cheek, showing that she was caring and nurturing, possibly to a fault. One such line signifies responsibility, but several multiplies the tendency to care for others to the point of selflessness.

If I had to guess her profession at a glance, I would have pegged her as a kindergarten teacher or a nurse—and very likely a mother. She was, indeed, the single mother of two school-age children. To support them, she worked as the head of the graphic design department at a museum. There were other department heads for editorial, production, and manufacturing, all reporting to the museum's chief of publications.

"As design jobs go, mine's not bad," she said. "We create the exhibition catalogs and things like cards and calendars for the gift shop. The work itself can be a little boring, but we deal with beautiful images. I'm not dissatisfied, but I do wonder if there's more to life."

Everything about her was oriented to the left, meaning that it was controlled by the right or emotional, creative, and imaginative side of her brain. Her hair was braided on the left side, the left side of her body was angled slightly forward as she faced me, and even her left front tooth stuck out a bit, overlapping the right. The front teeth reflect the ego. A prominent right front tooth would indicate the importance of logic and material things, while a more prominent left one, like hers, signified that feelings were all-important.

I told her about her leftward orientation, saying, "I can see that you're very emotional, warmhearted, and giving."

"Yes, that sounds right," she said.

She'd mentioned that, being in her late thirties, she was one of the older members of the publications staff, supervising a twenty-something team. "I bet everyone looks up to you as a role model and older sister, coming to you with their family conflicts, career questions, and romantic crises—all the problems of being young."

"Oh yes—the controlling parents, the passionate loves, the terrible heartbreaks. Starting out in life is so hard."

"You're too big-hearted to turn anyone away. Young people know you'll accept them, take care of them, even love them. But who plays that role for you? Who showers you with love?"

"My family's in Denmark, but I have my kids," she said. "Their love for me is boundless."

"Yes, of course, but children's love can be a one-way street. You're responsible for them, and they can't take care of you. For that, you need a loving adult. That's probably part of what you're missing when you want more in life. And what about creative work? You say your job is somewhat rewarding, if dull, but your goals are not your own. Maybe 'more to life' means cultivating your own art projects."

"I can't prioritize things like that right now," she said. "I have no time for myself."

"That's no doubt true for all working mothers, but for you it's a special challenge. People flock to you because they unconsciously recognize how emotionally generous you are. For you, giving is so natural that you consider receiving and creating to be luxuries, when for many of us they practically define 'more to life.'"

Since you've asked for advice, I have an idea for you. Finding time for yourself seems impossible, but there is a benefit to working with young people. You do much to nurture them: Why don't you ask them for help? You could set up a rotating schedule—one night each week, one of them would babysit for you. That night would be yours to do whatever you want—start dating, go out with friends, begin working on something. It would be built-in time for yourself."

"I never thought about that," she said. "My kids are in after-school programs, so I just pick them up after work. It's always tough to find people to babysit."

"You'd book this time as if it were a weekly event. Which it is—for you, a night with no responsibility for anyone else is a major event. If your staff can't do it, they may have friends who'd be interested. Young people always need money. It would be so easy for you to develop a whole network of babysitters you know and trust to make sure that you get your personal time one night a week."

Often the smartest people overlook the most obvious solutions. For givers, especially, it's hard to imagine being free of constraints and focused, even for one night, completely on themselves. But as I told this working mother, if you keep nurturing and giving without replenishing, eventually you'll have nothing left. You may feel fulfilled in the moment, but you may never achieve the "more to life" that definitely exists.

A No-Teamwork Team

The head of a financial services firm in Singapore asked me for help motivating his team. "I don't know what's up with them,"

he told me. "No matter how much I push, coax, and encourage, they aren't making their numbers. I'm tempted to dump them and bring in a fresh new batch."

"That sounds extreme."

He laughed. "I'm half kidding. Maybe you can figure them out," he said.

To start, I did brief readings with his eight top managers to weigh their strengths and weaknesses. I didn't spot a bad apple in the group. Then I spent a day observing them in action. All eight impressed me as intelligent and diligent, though uncertain of their priorities and a bit frustrated.

"So what's wrong?" the CEO asked. "How come they keep spinning their wheels?"

"I don't think it's them," I had to say. "I fear that you may be the problem."

"Me? How is that possible? I built this company from nothing."

"I believe it," I said. "But it takes different skills to empower others to achieve."

He was surprised when I told him that he wasn't meant to lead. "You're freedom-loving, creative, and impulsive. You have a good sense of people, so you're great at choosing staff. But your ideas get lost in translation. Your thinking is too complex for your team to follow. You don't know how to guide and support them."

"What makes you say that?"

For one thing, his face had no visible King elements. You can have leadership skills without being a King, but he was a Fire face, very driven and passionate. Because he could whip people into a fervor with his enthusiasm, he thought he was a leader. But a true leader doesn't just motivate the troops. Before he sends them into battle, a leader lays out a strategy, showing them the steps to achieve his vision. There are concrete goals in his rousing message.

My client was visionary enough to run a company but too "big picture" in his ideas to break them down for others. His very high forehead was hatched with lots of straight, unbroken lines, connoting not just thinking but zipping from start to finish in his thoughts, too quickly for his team to follow. His mouth was long but with the lips bunched up in the middle, typical of a secret keeper, not a communicator. His large nose had flared nostrils. Such nostrils convey a need to breathe, a wish for space, impatience with the tangle of routine. Even his wavy hair and his ears, with tips reaching higher than his eyes, indicated impetuous innovation, not corporate strategy.

"What can I do differently?" he asked.

"I don't think you want to act differently," I said. "The slog of day-to-day management would leave you bored and resentful. You could handle it, but I think you'd do better to hire a chief executive, someone better at offering guidance and setting goals. There are plenty of people who excel at that. They don't create so much as systematize, which is a skill in itself."

"You were smart enough to hire diligent workers—people who can execute your vision—but they can't find their way without an organizer-in-chief. That's just not you."

"Hmmm," he said. "I'm listening."

"Why force yourself to care about mundane procedures? Think about what you like to do best. Is it expanding into new markets? Is it dreaming up new directions for clients? Is it helping established industries innovate? What accomplishment would make you proudest? Shouldn't that be your focus?"

"Well . . ." he said.

"It's your company, so you can do what you want. Shouldn't it be the work that you enjoy?"

"I see your point," he conceded.

"Let's face it: you're not the kind of man who can fit inside a box—not even the box of a boss."

10

Health

For thousands of years, face reading has been used to diagnose health. Chapter 3 traces its development in the West from the time of Hippocrates, who was among the first to treat illness as a physical disorder rather than a spiritual condition. "Face mapping" has long been an important diagnostic tool both in India, where the five-thousand-year-old tradition of Ayurveda continues, and in China, where it remains one of the Four Pillars of Diagnosis of Traditional Chinese Medicine (TCM). In Chinese diagnosis, study of the tongue is especially important.

There are TCM charts—and today, even apps—showing which areas of the face are connected to internal organs. These charts may vary depending on the particular school of TCM. Changes in skin color or texture in a given area may suggest an imbalance in the related organ systems. Today, scientists in China are doing computer analyses to measure whether changes in facial coloration actually correspond to the traditional diagnoses. A three-thousand-year-old practice has catapulted into the digital age.

Obviously, it takes years of study to master the diagnostic methods of TCM. I'm not a TCM specialist but draw on the various face-reading traditions in which I'm trained. "The Face of Health" section in part III, "A Face-Reading Reference Guide," offers a face map and describes some of the health conditions detectable in the face.

One warning I always offer clients is "Beware of self-medication." I refer my clients to qualified health professionals, especially practitioners of integrative medicine, who are grounded in both conventional and alternative methods.

Green Eyes

I met my German face-reading master while I was studying nutrition, hoping to heal my debilitating health problems. As I described in chapter 2, it was a huge leap of faith to become his student because he warned, "Eric, it will cost you your belief system."

Of course, over the year and a half I spent with him, he did change my belief system, and for the better. But I was a little miffed, I have to confess, when the first toll he exacted was what little remained of my vanity.

For years, women I dated had told me that I had beautiful green eyes. I was rather proud of them, considering them my most unusual and possibly best feature. So when my teacher pointed out to the other students, "Eric has really strong green eyes," I was flattered.

"Thank you," I said.

"It's not a compliment," he replied. "It's a sign that there's too much acid in your body."

What? The master explained that true green eyes are rare and, interestingly, found less often in men than in women. Being born with them is not a sign of ill health, but he could tell that my eyes were naturally blue. That may have been true during childhood, but I had no idea when the color changed or even that such a change was possible. Research showed me that conditions like pregnancy, trauma, and viruses—even aging—can change eye color. So it's definitely a physical change that warrants attention. In my case, body chemistry was the issue.

Conventional science doesn't fully accept this notion, but there are many mysteries that it can't explain. For example, in one widely reported story, when a doctor, Ian Crozier, was treated for Ebola, the virus holed up in one of his eyes, which turned green. When he finally recovered, his eye reverted to blue—a miracle, in the Western medical view. For me, green eyes are a sign that my system is weak and needs to be bolstered through behavior and diet.

On the behavioral side, since I know that I'm vulnerable to stress, I take conscious steps to restore balance when my eyes look green. I resist overwork and excessive physical activity and, importantly, reject habits of mind, like negative thinking and rumination, that promote acidity.

As for food and drink, I avoid alcohol and coffee (my big temptation), as well as sugar, fried foods, and the like. When I look acidic, I eat "clean." With the right nutrition, our organs naturally cleanse us, though it doesn't hurt to help them out now and then by adding a little spirulina, chlorella, or ginger to a smoothie. Once or twice a year, I might spend a couple weeks doing an actual cleanse, with a restricted diet. This is my personal practice, which might not benefit someone with a different body chemistry. And when my equilibrium is restored, my eyes shine more blue.

Changing color is an uncommon and dramatic red flag, but the eyes signal even ordinary shifts in body chemistry. Look at the eyes of someone who's getting drunk—they sparkle as the person gets high-spirited. But the next day, in the throes of a hangover, the person's eyes are dull, as if a gray curtain has fallen over them. Years of heavy drinking or taking drugs will be reflected in the eyes, as will any other trauma, received or inflicted, like physical abuse.

Because the eyes are so directly connected to the brain, they're a good barometer of well-being. Observe your own eyes and notice changes. If they look grayish, if they itch, if the sclera (the white part) changes color or is threaded with red vessels, your equilibrium may be off. It's worth thinking about what's going on and how to get back in balance.

When I was in training, my master was painfully honest in noting the students' worst qualities. He'd tell me, "Eric, you're sarcastic. Sometimes you seem cynical and arrogant."

I could handle that criticism, which helped me overcome the less appealing aspects of my personality. But there was one judgment I couldn't bear. After remarking on the color of my eyes, my master perceived them as flat: "Your eyes don't shine anymore."

I think that's the worst thing a face reader can ever say. It means that your imagination, inspiration, and motivation, as well as your health, are failing—that your spirit is depleted. When my eyes began to glisten again, I knew that process of healing, physically and emotionally, was under way.

The Acid Test

When a friend and I were in London, we had a hankering for pizza, and someone steered us to a good place. It was tiny, run by Sicilian parents and their daughter, who looked to be in her early twenties. She would have looked more her age had she not had a Mountain face. Pear-shaped, with a forehead narrower than the jaws, which slopes back from the nose, a Mountain face is unusual in a women and rare in a woman so young.

As she took our order, we could hear her parents fighting in the kitchen. Since they were speaking Italian, we couldn't understand the words, but their wrath was clear. Her face bore no reaction—she didn't look apologetic or roll her eyes or even smile to acknowledge the commotion. When she delivered the order slip, we heard them yell at her, but when she brought our food, her face was impassive.

Luckily, the fight died down enough for us to eat in relative peace. When we left, we saw her perched outside on a little bench, smoking a cigarette. "Where are you from?" she asked.

As she and my friend began chatting, I had the chance to study her closely. Her eyes were almost obscured by a heavy black eyeliner, like kohl. But I could see swollen bags beneath them, as if she'd been crying all night or partying. When such bags persist, they show that the kidneys and bladder are doing a poor job of preventing fluid buildup. There were also pouchy little swellings to the left and right of her lower lip, suggesting weakness of the gallbladder. The corners of her mouth turned downward, confirming what we already had reason to suspect: that she was very unhappy.

"Why do you work here?" I asked her. "It seems difficult."

"My parents need my support," she said.

"Need it or just expect it? The place seems small enough for them to manage."

She acknowledged this was true. "I'm ambitious," she told me. "I'm saving up to go to college. It's hard to make much money in such a little restaurant, but I figure I can stick it out."

That was a typical Mountain face statement. The Mountain face always takes the "long path," as Chinese face readers put it. Their eyes are on the future, not the present, so they put things off and become late bloomers. I explained face reading and the qualities of the Mountain face to her.

"You have the endurance and patience to stick it out," I said, "but it's taking a physical toll. Normally, especially at your age, detox organs like your kidneys and gallbladder sweep acidity from the body, but you're collecting it. I see that in your face."

I pointed to two moles I spotted above her eyebrows. "These moles, one on the left, and one on the right, are your second eyes. You line your eyes with black to hide what they express and also to keep from acknowledging what you see. But having second eyes means that you're intuitive and empathetic. You can't help absorbing feelings, especially the conflict between your parents. You can't deny how much it hurts you.

"These are the emotions that are causing your acidity."

She was listening carefully.

"So, you might be destined to take the long path, but you don't have to take it all the time," I said. "If you take the long path in a better job, at least there's a chance you'll reach your destination. The longer you procrastinate, being a Mountain face, the less likely you are to make any headway at all."

By this point, I was starting to think I was foisting unsolicited advice on a stranger. But I'd been so struck by the sense that she was trapped—and that, in a Mountain face way, might just bide her time rather than free herself—that I had to speak. She did seem appreciative and thoughtful. I still wonder where her path led.

The Bully's Secret

While I was working with my German master, I recovered my health, but it took me a while to gain the discipline to cope with skeptics. I'm not proud of this story, but it was a meaningful, instructive mistake.

At a health fair where I was reading, a man impatiently jostled his way to my table, trailed by his embarrassed wife. In Germany I describe him as a real Schwarzenegger type, and everyone

laughs. They know the profile—burly, swaggering, belligerent, and eager to intimidate me, a much smaller man. "I don't believe in this crap," he began, "but you impressed my wife, and I want to prove her wrong. If you're so great, let's see if you can spot the one problem I have."

His bellowing attracted a little knot of onlookers, which made my job harder. Willing myself to concentrate, I switched on my lamp and trained it on his face. The first thing I noticed was his chin, which was red and threaded with visible vessels. There was also a deep horizontal wrinkle at the break between the chin itself and the lower lip. It too was deep red, a sign of inflammation.

That part of his face was related to the lower part of his body, especially the colon, but he wasn't suffering like a man whose guts were on fire. So I concluded that the guy had a long history of hemorrhoids. An introvert's hemorrhoids might bleed inside the rectum and be less detectable. But in such a loudmouth, I was sure that they bled on the outside and were no doubt quite painful.

"So?" he challenged me.

"If I had huge bleeding hemorrhoids like you do," I said, "I might be just as pushy."

The spectators laughed, and a few even clapped. He pushed through them and slunk away, with his wife scolding, "See! I told you he was real!"

For a while I felt triumphant. I had a new superpower, and it worked—it put Goliath in his place. But on the drive home, I had to admit, "Eric, that was not cool." I should have been empathetic, telling the guy, "I see your problem, but let's discuss it in private." Instead, I'd embarrassed him to punish his arrogance and, I confess, to show off.

My master had warned me to avoid such encounters. "If a skeptic is curious, you can try to convince him. But a bully—just let him go. Don't accept his challenge even if you're sure to win. He won't admit that he lost, and winning might cost you. In a power game, no one comes out the victor."

I'd turned a challenge into a power game. I'd betrayed my gift by using it not to advise but to stoke my ego. What had I gained but a few laughs? Not a converted skeptic or the humble satisfaction of helping him. So, in winning, I had lost.

It was a powerful lesson.

The Support System

The spine is our body's literal support system. It holds us erect and enables flexible movements. It houses the spinal cord, the bundle of nerve fibers sending messages to and from the brain and branching out to control the body's functions. Since the spine plays so

many different and important roles, it's not surprising that many people suffer from back pain, which may be hard to diagnose or heal. Often, they turn to painkillers, which introduce their own set of problems.

A Dutch woman in her thirties consulted me about her mysterious but crippling backaches. She'd made the rounds of doctors and had a battery of screening tests. When the results proved negative, all that the doctors could recommend was massage—which did help, but the effects didn't last. "Can you see anything?" she asked. "Maybe some problem the doctors missed?"

Her face showed the usual back-pain marker, lines across the bridge of the nose. The higher the lines, the farther up the back the problem lies. But she also had a horizontal line between her nose and upper lip. That can signify great sorrow, but I had to interpret it in the light of other factors I saw: not just the lines on the bridge of her nose but also jowls, too droopy for someone her age, indicating trouble with the connective tissues of her face. The final confirmation was her coloring. Her complexion was pale, but with an ashy tinge. "You look seriously deficient in calcium," I told her. "Enough that I worry that you may have osteoporosis."

"What?" she said. "I thought you had to be old to get that."

It is unusual for a young woman to have osteoporosis, which is probably why the doctors didn't think to check for it. I advised her to get a bone density test.

The bone density test confirmed that she had osteoporosis, and she began a course of treatment and exercise. "Finally, I'm recovering mobility," she told me. "I'm getting a new lease on life."

The Weight of the World

Most men first encounter face reading in a business context, when I consult for corporations. Otherwise, the men I see tend to be referred by women. So I was surprised when a man in his fifties, who looked like the managerial type, dropped in without an appointment. "I saw your office sign," he said. "I wonder if you can help me."

He didn't say why he needed help, so I surmised that he was in physical pain. For one thing, the lines across the bridge of his nose, suggesting a bad back, were fiery red, indicating an active problem. He had awkward posture because his left shoulder seemed to have limited motion. His right pupil was small, implying an analytic nature, but the left one was huge. "You have back pain radiating from your left shoulder," I said, "confirmed by the strong emotion, which could be pain, that your dilated left pupil reflects."

"Wow, you're right," he told me. "On and off, my left shoulder is incredibly painful. I've had X-rays, bone density tests—you name it—that look normal. Massages and things like liniments help, but nothing solves the problem."

"What do you carry on your left side?" I asked.

"I don't use a backpack or anything like that."

"Emotionally, I mean. The left, or heart, side governs emotions and feelings."

"Well, I've always been a giver," he began. The second of four sons, with a remote, withdrawn father and unreliable older brother, he'd borne the whole emotional burden of his family. He'd married and had a child with a nervous, dependent woman. "But since my dad died, my mother expects me to keep her company and to manage her chores and finances. My wife resents those demands because, with our child grown and gone, she feels lonely and abandoned. They've never liked each other, but now they compete fiercely, with my wife calling my mother an abusive manipulator, and my mother saying that my wife is controlling and clingy. There may be an element of truth in their words, but I can't stand being at the center of a tug-of-war."

"So you try to please both," I said. "Which is impossible."

"Oh yeah," he said. "So what should I do?"

Of course, I couldn't help him choose between his mother and his wife. But I did offer him a strategy I learned from my Chinese master. We'd been sitting in my master's kitchen, which was his command post, when a man in his early twenties dropped in. "Are you my next client?" the master asked.

"Yes," the man said. He seemed deferential.

But my master was unimpressed. Pointing to the door, he said, "You—go! Go!"

This was rude even for an imperious Chinese master. The man left in shock. By then I was no longer a student, so I could ask, "What were you thinking? Why be so high-handed and shoo him away?"

"Go ahead and read him," my master said, "if you want to waste energy." He'd somehow ascertained that the guy wasn't worth the effort—that he was too immature or wouldn't properly grasp or respect what he heard. Puzzling over the dismissal, I wondered whether the master, losing stamina at his advanced age, was reserving his gifts for those who could truly benefit.

It also struck me that the dismissed client had actually gained by the rejection. He would wonder, "What's wrong with me? Why did he treat me that way?" That would make him reflect, to try to understand—and work to overcome—the shortcomings that the master detected. So, in effect, he'd been assessed by a great master, one of the most prominent face-reading authorities in Hong Kong, without paying for it.

That story held a lesson, I told my client. By dismissing someone who might tax his energy, my master shifted the burden of proving worthiness to the client. Had he explained why he was rejecting the man, he would have gotten an argument—"I'm not too young! I will understand!"—and might have been stuck reading someone who now resented him, compounding the waste of energy.

"These two demand your energy without investing their love in you. They don't care how hard you work to please them. Any attention you give one becomes a weapon against the other. So stop trying to satisfy either of them. Do the opposite—simply retreat and refuse to do what they ask. Let them come to you not with demands on your time but by making the effort to win you back. They have to approach you with compassion for your efforts and with gratitude for what you do. Otherwise, none of you wins. They both feel deprived, since they don't appreciate what they get, and you feel torn in half. It's time to switch the energy flow from them to you."

The man listened to me closely and even took notes. He left standing a little straighter, with more assurance in his step. Sometimes, when people have undiagnosable pain, it's "all in their heart" instead of "all in their head."

Why We Gain Weight

Since body and mind are intertwined, it's not surprising that both contribute to any given health condition. Rarely, though, are the effects as traceable as they were with one of my health spa clients. A British woman in her fifties, she had come to lose weight after

trying a dozen or more fad diets. At first, I referred her to the nutritionists, saying, "They'll do what I can't, which is help you map out a concrete eating plan."

She planned to consult them but wanted a reading to ascertain why all the diets didn't work. Even at first glance, her face showed signs of trouble metabolizing carbohydrates, especially when consumed with fats. She had puffy pouches at her jawline and beneath her lower lip, as well as skin slackness (the beginning of jowls) and spots of brownish pigmentation. Vertical lines in her fingernails confirmed this impression. "You need to avoid foods like french fries or even bread and butter," I said. "The carb–fat combination is bad for you. In fact, I'd stay away from white potatoes and white flour and choose complex carbohydrates, like whole grains."

I could also see that she loved red wine. The "red wine face"—different from the typical face of an alcoholic—has characteristics that, interestingly, don't show up in those who over-indulge in white wine. Heavy drinkers of red wine often have pronounced vertical lines between the eyes, like thinker lines but with pigmented spots between them. Such lines are not enough to identify a red wine drinker unless they appear with other signs. These include droopy upper eyelids, lots of fine lines and en-larged pores below the eyes, a reddish cast to the cheeks and dry wrinkled skin around the cheekbones, and very deep lines running from the nose to the mouth. The box "The Face of Excess" shows the facial evidence associated with some of the substances we consume.

Her red cheeks and the leg cramps she said she experienced at night suggested that, like many who overdo it with alcohol, she was deficient in magnesium. With that, I could have finished the reading. The indications in her face were so obvious that it was one of the quickest I've ever done. Any competent nutritionist would probably give her a diet that addressed the problems I'd uncovered.

But then I was drawn to a mole, like a dark skin tag, just below the outer tip of one eyebrow. Of course, as my masters taught, if your intuition draws you to a feature, even seemingly random, pay attention—it's related to the client's issue. So I consulted a destiny map, a Chinese chart that identifies 108 points on the face linked to the years of a woman's life. Any anomalous mark (a mole, a scar) appearing near a point signifies a momentous year—not good or bad, but simply important. Because there are several charts, all of which require intensive study to interpret well, I am not reproducing them here.

The mole was in a spot associated with the woman's thirty-fourth year. "The fact that you can't lose weight might be connected to that age," I told her. "Did something happen when you were thirty-four?"

She started crying, which has physical as well as emotional benefits. Tears detoxify the body. That's why it's best to let them fall, not choke them back, so they can help release acidity. So I waited long minutes for her sobs to subside before saying, "You must have gone through a tough time."

"Yes, that year my little daughter was hit by a car in London. She died, and I couldn't stand England anymore. Or even Europe. So I came to Asia, where I had some possible clients for my event-planning business. Now it's booming, to the point that all I do is work and sleep. It's a mixed blessing."

"Is the girl's father in the picture?" I had no idea whether she'd been married, and she didn't enlighten me.

"No, he's still in London. Or so I believe. We're not in touch."

Then she wanted to hear my advice. "But not on nutrition," she said with a smile.

I had to explain, as usual, that I could offer insight but not guidance. But I did say, "You have such intense unresolved feelings about London that it seems you should go back there, at least for a visit. Maybe you need to touch base with your ex. Maybe you need to see the site of the accident. I don't think you'll find peace until you confront the situation and the emotions you fled."

I urged her to find a therapist to help work through those feelings. "In a big city like London, you should find someone good."

And maybe, when she stopped swallowing her pain, she'd have better success at losing weight.

The Sneaky Vegan

Many couples consult me about infertility because, all too often, it's hard to pinpoint the cause. They hope that face reading will detect a problem missed by invasive medical tests. Sometimes, I can spot a mineral deficiency or suggest a change of diet, which might help. But with one couple I met, the source of infertility quickly became obvious.

They were yoga teachers who'd seen me profiled in a major magazine. Both longtime vegans, they looked to be in perfect physical health—and, in fact, were exceptionally attractive. But, as they explained, they'd been trying for three years to conceive. They'd made the rounds of doctors and had all the tests, which came back normal. "And your sex life—is that normal?" I asked.

They both looked sheepish before the wife said, "Well, no. We used to be wild about each other, but over the past few years we've lost our passion."

"So, is this a mental problem?" I said. "I'm not a therapist. Have you considered counseling or even a tantric yoga expert?"

"We just want to know what our faces show," she told me. "Maybe they hold an answer."

At that point, I wondered if they were looking for some missing mystical connection, like diverging destinies or mismatched past lives. Face reading has nothing to do with such spiritual notions. It's firmly grounded in this world, in patterns of observation established over the millennia.

But I gave it a try. The wife had a Jade face, with a delicate nose, an appealing gaze, and a wide mouth with ample lips. It was the face of a lover, a giver—a good mother. The way her mouth moved was not sensual and welcoming, though, but pinched and unexpressive. Clearly, there was an emotional blockage that corresponded to her lack of passion. When I explained this, she was disappointed. She'd hoped for some big revelation that would help her get pregnant. "I'm going to head to the restroom and maybe get a cup of tea," she said, "while you read my husband."

I'd sensed that the husband wasn't eager for a reading. He had a King face—that of a leader, of a nurturing caretaker—which would predispose him to fatherhood. As we talked, his mouth, unlike his wife's, was very animated. He was as emotionally lively as she was constrained.

Why? I wondered. I leaned in closer, to appraise him more carefully, and then I caught it—a strong whiff of testosterone. Every sensory impression I get factors into a reading, and this was an important clue. There are only a few reasons why you smell testosterone on a man.

So I asked, "Did you come here straight from a workout?"

"No, we weren't at the studio today. We came from home."

"Have you been eating red meat? I know you're vegan, but if you crave a steak, it's no crime to sneak one now and then."

"No way," he said. "It's been years since I've thought about meat."

"Okay," I told him. "Then I have a problem. Your wife's passion is stifled, but yours is fully stoked. You're living your emotions, but she's not part of it."

When his gaze dropped to the floor, shifting from left to right—a sign of guilt—I knew that he was embroiled in an affair. I fully expected him to deny it. Instead, he stood up and looked me straight in the eyes, without a word. That was a mute cry: "Help me."

It touched my heart that he didn't even try to lie. Obviously, he cared deeply for his wife. It seemed likely that he was infatuated, not in love, with the other woman, or perhaps he was seeing several.

His wife's suppressed emotions made sense in this context. She thought they were trying to conceive, but they weren't having sex. She had to wonder why. She was probably swallowing hurt and anger over his distraction or his outright rejection, whether or not she suspected his affair.

"I can't tell you what to do about your marriage," I said. "But it doesn't seem fair to have her hoping for a pregnancy that you either don't want or are too worn out to make happen."

It was a Friday, so I asked him, "Do you know she's coming Monday for nutrition and fertility consultation? I can't lie to her. Why don't you talk to her over the weekend, or else I'll have to tell her the truth."

"Okay, I'll take care of it," he said.

I assume that he did because she didn't show up Monday.

Sometime later, I came across a flyer for their studio that listed both their names. I took that as a good sign.

Snow White and the Shining Face

I've encountered some very interesting challenges in my nutrition readings. I say "challenges" because clients often come to me when conventional medicine can't pinpoint the cause of their symptoms. Making the connection between nutrition and health is still a newish idea in Western medicine. Alternative medical systems such as Traditional Chinese Medicine, Ayurveda, and homeopathy, which do recognize the linkage, remain controversial; and the remedies they offer, being unsupported by large-scale studies, cannot be sold as treatments and, unlike drugs, are not regulated. I'm a face reader, not a doctor, so if I do gain insight into a nutritional issue like a deficiency, I advise clients to seek out health professionals, like integrative medicine doctors with knowledge of both allopathic and alternative systems, to assess and treat them.

But sometimes a change of diet alone can make a difference.

One July, a young woman came to see me because she was freezing. It was a typical summer in Karlsruhe, with temperatures hovering above 80 degrees. "Most people are complaining about the heat," she said. "But I can't get warm, even in a sweater." She'd been to various doctors, but so far nothing had helped.

"Do you have other symptoms?" I asked. "Like fatigue or inflammation?"

"Oh yes, I'm exhausted," she told me. "It seems that I'm always getting bladder infections. And I feel like an old woman, so stiff I can hardly move."

At that point, I was puzzled. I had a hunch that her problem was diet-related, but since she was so young—barely in her twenties—her face didn't hold the clues I normally see in an older person. But then I spotted a stripe that was milky white below her lower eyelid. Studying her more closely, I noticed that her whole face had a ghostly, translucent cast and was shades paler than her throat. "Would you mind pushing your sleeve up to the shoulder?" I asked.

When she did, I could see that her arm was as milky white as her face. This was a syndrome—sometimes called alabaster skin—that was recognized as far back as the time of Hippocrates. It was indeed diet related, likely produced by the deficiency of a mineral salt in the potassium family. Taking it as a supplement could be dangerous and would require the supervision of a skilled health professional. But I could suggest some foods that might help, including sunflower seeds, lentils, potatoes, tomatoes, grapefruit, and olives.

I'm happy to say that the change of diet worked. Her joint pain eased, and she started to regain her energy. She no longer bundled up in the heat. She still had the alabaster skin on her face and arms, so she wasn't completely in balance, but her most worrisome symptoms had resolved.

Another client had a similar whiteness but, strangely, it was reflective. I'm not talking about oily skin, but a stretch of the face, running from the tip of the nose out to the ear, that had a smooth white, mirrorlike sheen. The areas from the corners of the eyes to the ear were the glossiest.

She hadn't come with specific complaints, but the milky coloration on her face was so odd that I couldn't help asking, "Does your skin itch? Have you been losing hair?"

"Yes," she said. "I itch a lot, and my hair has been coming out in handfuls. I've been worried about it."

These symptoms suggested a deficiency of silica, a mineral that's not so easy to find in food. Possible sources range from oatmeal, wheat bread, and even beer to dandelions, figs, and asparagus. But since Silicea, a silica compound, is used in homeopathy, I thought that, instead of doing a hit-and-miss food trial, she might benefit from consulting a naturopathic physician. With his help, she got her minerals in balance, so her itching and hair loss subsided.

The Gray-Eyed Night Owl

A young man I encountered in my hometown of Karlsruhe asked a strange question: "Does my face scare you?"

I was surprised because the idea never occurred to me, but he explained that he'd been looking for jobs waiting tables. One restaurant manager rejected him, saying, "You look a bit too menacing to appeal to customers." Then he asked someone out on a date, who said no and told a friend that he seemed "scary." When questioned, his friend admitted, "Well, yes, your face might seem a little frightening to someone who doesn't know you."

The guy wasn't covered with tattoos or piercings, which some might find scary, and his expression didn't strike me as angry or aggressive. But he did have one unusual feature: wide dark-grayish lines below his eyes. It looked as if someone had swabbed his lower eyelids with a paintbrush.

"The only thing that frightens me is how little you sleep," I said. "You look dog-tired. Do you ever get to bed before dawn?"

"Not much. It varies, but I'm a night owl."

He also had an air of restless lethargy, as if he were too on edge to relax but too exhausted to take action. I could imagine that someone might find his energy confusing and, coupled with his grayish eyelids, possibly threatening.

"So you're definitely not a morning person," I said—he laughed—"and probably not a self-starter. Do you need someone to motivate you and tell you what to do?"

"Yes," he admitted. "I guess it's just my personality."

"I don't think so. I think you lack iron. We need it to boost our immune system and also for vitality."

Our bodies use iron to make hemoglobin in our red blood cells, which carry oxygen from our lungs to our muscles and other organs, as well as collect carbon dioxide and deliver it to the lungs, where we expel it by exhaling. Obviously, these are critical functions. Globally, lack of iron is one of the most common mineral deficiencies.

But that doesn't mean that we can just pop supplements. Menstruating women lose iron every month, but in the rest of us, with no way to escape, it can build up, causing a condition called hemochromatosis, with dangerous or even fatal effects, including impotence in men and liver damage. That's why, in the old days, bloodletting was used to alleviate ailments thought to be caused by excess iron in the blood.

Getting iron from foods is much safer. It's most easily absorbed from animal products such as shellfish, organ meats like liver, red meats, and dark turkey meat, but it's also found in quinoa, tofu, legumes like black beans and lentils, pumpkin seeds, and in broccoli and dark greens like spinach.

What I suspected might be helpful to my client was a homeopathic compound, ferrum phosphoricum, taken before bedtime. It would promote sleep, while an iron-rich dinner, like liver, might still be digesting. But not being a naturopath, I referred him to an integrative medicine doctor for evaluation and treatment.

But then I told him, "Whatever you do, you need to get to bed at a regular time, no later than ten. No more staying up till four or five."

"What? Why?" He was spluttering.

"Because you need unbroken, deeper sleep, which is harder to get when you're working against the body's normal cycle, keyed to daylight. Also, to get rid of those dark lines and your lethargy, you need to detox. The detox organs work at night, not at the crack of dawn. For a few weeks at least, you have to be strict about it to retrain yourself.

"Once you've reset your body clock, you can stay out once in a while, maybe till one. But don't make it a habit. Your energy and concentration will improve. And your eyelids won't be gray but will reflect the person you are."

The Blink of an Eye

The manager of a top English soccer team called me about one of his players. "How soon can you fly here?" he asked. "Because I have a player who can't do television. He blinks like crazy in front of the camera. People are starting to talk about it, which is embarrassing."

"Is it like a nervous tic?" I said.

"That's what the doctors think. It's only in one eye. It's distracting, when normally he's a great spokesman for the team. And it's the wrong kind of publicity."

I couldn't get away as soon as the manager wanted, so I asked him to send videos. Certainly, I knew and admired the player. Watching him speak, I could see how pronounced the blink was. In every postgame interview, it showed up.

At the bottom of the stack, like an afterthought, was a video shot in a TV studio. Four commentators, two on each side of the player, were discussing his thoughts on the league. Though he was the focus of four questioners, the player was at ease and undaunted by the setting—the bright lights, the techs and equipment crowding the space, and the multiple cameras. He was fully engaged—and not blinking.

Why? I wondered, peering at his face. If nerves were the problem, the studio session should have really set him off.

Shifting back and forth between the videos, I saw the difference. In the studio, the player had an even skin tone, but in all the postgame interviews, his cheeks were red. He'd cooled down from exertion and excitement of the game, so that didn't explain the redness. Between the twitching eyelid and the ruddy cheeks, I surmised that his problem was lack of magnesium.

It made sense. The player threw himself into the game with intense force and concentration, so by the final whistle he had completely exhausted his magnesium stores. Lack of magnesium makes people crave sweets, coffee, or energy drinks; get headaches and muscle cramps; or, because magnesium helps with nervous system function, develop twitches.

I explained my theory to the manager and suggested a way to test it. After a game, the player could take a supplement as recommended by a doctor—dosing yourself with any supplement can be risky—or eat magnesium-rich foods like pumpkin seeds, almonds, cashews, peanuts, or even a green smoothie made with spinach and kale. He'd have to give the mineral time to kick in, perhaps by taking a shower before talking to the press. Very likely, he could then give interviews without blinking.

The strategy worked. The player went on to give effective interviews for the rest of the season. Today, some years later, he is retired from the team and—in quite a transformation—has become a television sportscaster.

The Red Nose

I never thought much about why my friend had a red nose. I was aware of it, but with someone so familiar, you tend to focus on the eyes and less on other features unless they change. But one day, he asked, "Do I look like a drunk to you? Because that's what people assume."

"I've never seen you drink much, so it didn't cross my mind. How long has your nose been red?"

"Maybe ten years. I wasn't born this way. But now I'm starting to wonder about the cause."

The tip of his nose was bright red. That suggested that his stomach, for whatever reason, was inflamed. Studying his face, I could barely trace his nasolabial lines, the ones running from the edges of the nostrils to the corners of the lips. They were that indistinct, which is very unusual for a man in his thirties. Their faintness confirmed my diagnosis of a distressed stomach.

I knew that gastritis, a stomach infection caused by a virus or bacteria (especially *Helicobacter pylori,* the organism that can lead to ulcers), can be chronic, but it wouldn't last ten years without symptoms. "Are you taking any medications?" I asked, because some can irritate the stomach lining. He wasn't. So the cause was most likely his diet.

"What are your favorite foods?" I asked.

Everything he named was an animal protein: cheese, eggs, sausage and bacon, lamb chops, burgers, and steaks. Depending on which fad diet you believe in, what he ate was an inspiration or a nightmare. His idea of vegetables was french fries or baked potatoes slathered in butter.

"Your digestive system needs a break," I told him. "Your nose shows that you're out of balance."

He looked worried. "I'm not going to tell you to give things

The Face of Excess

Our faces reflect our nutritional status and how well we metabolize whatever we ingest. So it's not surprising that they also offer clues to our overindulgences and other less-than-healthy habits. What follows are a few examples of the substances that, if overconsumed, leave evidence in our faces. When I see these signs, I suggest that clients slowly cut back on excesses and, in some cases, add supportive foods to their diets. The "Minerals" and "Metabolism" sections of Part III, "A Face-Reading Reference Guide," offer more information on food and micronutrients.

- *Alcohol.* Most of us recognize the face of alcoholism: bloated and puffy, with enlarged pores and broken capillaries, a flushed appearance or red skin blotches, and bloodshot eyes with red circles.
- *Red Wine.* Those who overconsume red wine over a long period may have characteristics different from those of the typical alcoholic: pronounced lines between the eyes with spots between the lines; enlarged pores and dry skin below the eyes, with many fine wrinkles; droopy eyelids; very deep lines running from the nose to the mouth; and dry reddish cheeks with a crosshatching of fine lines. Just one or two of these signs doesn't mark someone as a red wine drinker, but a combination is often the tip-off. Overindulgence in white wine, for some reason, doesn't seem to show up the same way in the face.
- *Refined Carbohydrates.* Wheat products are often the culprit. I don't know whether gluten or something else in wheat is the reason, but I often observe signs of excessive consumption in France, where people eat a lot of bread, and Italy, where they eat pasta. These are different from signs like puffiness at the jawline that indicate metabolic weakness with carbohydrates. The signs of overconsumption of refined wheat products include dark patches around the chin, on

the forehead, or in the cheeks, along with dark clogged pores or blackheads not related to the hormone changes of adolescence.

- *Sugar.* Heavy sugar intake over the years is often signaled by thin, deep lines and wrinkles on the upper forehead. The closer to the hairline they appear, the more sugar the person has consumed. Some Chinese face readers view this as a chicken-and-egg situation because lots of forehead lines are the mark of an idealistic, creative, imaginative person. Creators burn a lot of energy. So, which came first? A love of sugar, expressed in forehead lines, or heavy mental activity, requiring the quick energy boost of sugar?

  Other signs of sugar dependence are a gaunt look (sucked-in cheeks with a grayish-white tinge); thin and sagging skin below the eyes and over the cheekbones, producing crow's-feet; and, often, pimples scattered across the face.

- *Fried Foods.* For some of us, fried foods are just as addicting as sugar. Overindulgence makes the face sallow and shiny, with a greasy film that makes it hard for the skin to eliminate waste. When people cut back on fried foods, they often look a few years younger because the skin can renew itself.

- *Dairy Products.* People whose diets are heavy on milk, cheese, yogurt, butter, and the like often have pimples concentrated on the chin or scattered across the cheeks. Their cheeks tend to be pale, rather than rosy and healthy looking. Their upper eyelids are often swollen, and dark lines and circles may appear under the eyes. These changes very likely reflect the presence of hormones in dairy products, whether naturally occurring or fed to cows to boost milk production.

- *Red Meat.* If you look at middle-aged American and European men side by side, there's an obvious difference in their faces. More of the American faces are fleshy and bulldog-like, which I believe can be attributed to diet. American men, especially, eat a lot more red meat than most Europeans, which may cause their faces to balloon. You rarely see a passionate steak eater with a slender face.

American meat contains both natural hormones and a variety of added synthetic ones that have been banned for decades in many European countries. These hormones may play a role in the difference in American faces. On both continents, the heaviest meat eaters tend to have a range of problems with their colons and digestion that are recognizable to face readers.

- *Salt.* People who eat a lot of salt retain water, which shows up as swelling in the face, especially in the thin skin around the eyes. Bags under the eyes are often a sign of kidney and bladder weakness and may improve when people cut back on salt.

- *Smoking.* Smoking cigarettes not only affects the heart and lungs but can also add years to the face. Because smoking deprives the skin of oxygen and nutrients, it can alter skin coloration, leaving some pale and sallow and others with an uneven, blotchy tone. The four thousand chemicals in cigarettes degrade collagen and elastin, the fibers that give skin its strength and pliability. The result is sagging skin, especially under the eyes, and deep wrinkles, including crow's-feet and pronounced vertical lines around the lips. Among smoking's more serious effects on the face are cataracts, or cloudy areas on the retinas of the eyes, and oral and skin cancers.

- *Veganism.* It's easy to spot vegans who carefully balance their diets because they usually have amazing skin, glowing with health. Some look a decade or more younger than they are. But quite often I see vegans, especially those who give up animal products for philosophical rather than health reasons, who show all the hallmarks of consuming junk food—sugar, fat, salt, and refined carbohydrates.

up," I assured him. "That's between you and your doctor, based on your blood tests. But try this: three times a year, for two full weeks, go vegan and eat no animal products at all."

"What will I be able to eat?" he said. "I'm not a tofu and seaweed guy."

"You'll experiment. I think you'll discover a lot of new foods you didn't even know you liked."

That's what happened. Not only did his red nose fade but he found that he actually enjoyed the challenge. "It's not how I want to live all the time," he said, "but those vegan weeks really help me. Now I feel great. Better, lighter."

Runner's Face

"Runner's face" isn't a face-reading term, but in recent years a number of clients have asked about it. Apparently, some believe that running shakes your face, breaking down collagen and making skin sag; burns off fat and hollows your face, so you look like a skeleton; or ages you by deepening wrinkles. To some extent, these beliefs are true. The operative words are "to some extent."

People at midlife, especially women, who've trained hard for years are vulnerable to runner's face. That was the case with the American woman at a Hong Kong spa who introduced me to the expression. Though she was fifty, seeing her from the back, you'd think she was an athletic college student. Her body was that taut and slim. But if she turned around, you'd be shocked by her deeply sunken eyes and concave cheeks, each striped with a few wrinkles, like the gills of a shark. The wrinkles were fairly new, and she asked, "Did I get these lines from running? In other words, do I have runner's face?"

She told me about her lifestyle. For the past six years, she'd run five or six miles a day and had sharply reduced the carbo-hydrates in her diet. She pretty much subsisted on fish, chicken breasts, eggs, and vegetables, with minimal fats.

"That's pretty severe," I said.

"Well, it works for me. I'm proud of my discipline. And, come on, how many women over forty have a body like mine?"

"Your body represents you," I told her, "but your face expresses you. Are you willing to sacrifice what makes you most attractive—your self-expression—just to be thin?"

She looked disappointed that I didn't praise her self-control or her slenderness.

"Doing high-impact exercise every day is bound to affect your face," I said. Skin doctors consider a degree of jarring exercise beneficial because it boosts circulation. But too much, in some people, including my client, causes sagging or concave cheeks. Genetics plays a role in the way the body stays toned and distributes fat. Sunscreen can help prevent wrinkles. Nutrition, which is highly individual, is also a huge factor.

"I'm not saying that you can't run, but you do need to change your diet."

"Why?" she said. "What could be wrong with lean proteins and vegetables?"

"Nothing," I told her. "Some people flourish on a high-protein diet, but you need a different balance. Other women your age can work out every day and not get such skeletal faces."

I suspected that my client had a protein-metabolism disorder, based on the extreme angularity of her face and the new wrinkles. The "Metabolism" section of Part III, "A Face-Reading Reference Guide," offers more information on such conditions. A few questions confirmed my diagnosis.

"Do you often have diarrhea?"

She nodded. "And how about whitish pimples on your back?"

"How did you know I have them?"

"Those are signs of detoxing. When the body has more of a substance than it can handle—in your case, protein—it tries to expel it as fast as possible. Diarrhea is efficient and quick. Your skin, which is our largest detoxifying organ, tries to sweat out the excess, clogging the pores and creating pimples."

"Hmmm . . ." she said.

"And the intensity of your workouts—running five or six miles every day—isn't doing you much good either. Again, some people benefit from intensity, which helps balance them. But you're tipping the scales too far. The body craves equilibrium, not extremes."

"What makes you think it's not good for me?"

"In Chinese face reading, those new lines on your cheeks relate to the front lines on the battlefield. They show you're in a struggle for power or authority. What are you fighting?"

She was wearing a wedding ring. "Does your husband want you to be thin?"

"Not necessarily," she said. "He thinks my face looks old. But I see him staring at young Chinese women on the street, who are so tiny. If I comment on it, he gets prickly and says I'm imagining things."

"So fear keeps you running. You think you have to fight for him, though you're not sure his attention is straying. Maybe being on the front lines, fighting, running, always pushing yourself, is not your nature. You might be forcing yourself into a body, like a costume, that's right for some people, but not for you."

I sent her to the spa's nutritionists to rebalance her diet and urged her to vary her workouts—run four days a week, then do something else like yoga or dance for flexibility. Or just relax.

"No more extremes," I said. "Give yourself some freedom. Including freedom from fear."

The Blue Nose

Detecting a major health issue presents a significant challenge, both philosophical and moral, for a face reader. I've said often in this book that we're observers, not life coaches, career or marriage counselors, or mental or physical healers. We're diagnosticians only to the extent that our long-codified traditions, training, and, importantly, individual intuition allow us to interpret the signs in a face. In many places, the law prohibits us from offering medical advice. So what do we do when we're confronted with mortal illness?

That was the situation I faced with a sixty-something German man whose wife sent him for a nutrition reading. He'd been having terrible stomach pains, with no evident cause. I was immediately drawn to his nose. The tip, which is associated with the stomach, was only slightly red. Darker red might indicate alcoholism or, as in the case of my ruddy-nosed close friend, some kind of chronic stomach inflammation. The tip wasn't thickened, as we often see in connoisseurs, frequent indulgers in fine food and drink (a good example is Gérard Depardieu's large, fleshy nose). An irregularity I did see was blue and red veins snaking up the sides of the nostrils toward the bridge of the nose. That was worrisome.

While the tip of the nose reflects the stomach, the nose itself is related to the lungs. One or even a few signs don't add up to a firm conclusion, but unexpected prominent bluish veins warrant suspicion. The man had a troubling mix of symptoms—an air of unwellness overall, a pale complexion, and sunken temples, along with blue veins. I was forced to grapple with the likelihood that he had lung cancer.

"Do you smoke?" I asked.

"Why? The pain is in my stomach."

"Because nicotine and other chemicals in cigarettes, through your saliva, irritate the digestive tract. Smoking weakens the muscle between the stomach and esophagus, leading to conditions like heartburn and acid reflux. It's also a big risk factor in colon cancer. So I think your stomach pain may be more related to smoking than to your diet."

He seemed surprised. I gave him some tips on stomach-soothing foods and again urged him to quit smoking.

Now what? At the time, I'd been a face reader for only two years and was trying hard to adhere to my training. One rule my masters had strictly emphasized was, *Don't answer a question you're not asked.* In other words, don't impose your opinion on someone and change his nutrition reading to a health consultation. Also, though I had faith in my training, I was not a doctor who could order the medical tests a client in the West would expect when receiving such a grave verdict.

Maybe he was even being treated for cancer. But what if he didn't know? I was still struggling with the question when he rose to thank me, extending his hand as a good-bye. I shook it and said, with a controlled note of urgency, "Oh, one more thing—once a year, starting now, be sure to be examined by a pulmonologist."

"Seriously?" he said. "I barely know what a pulmonologist is. No one ever told me that."

"It's just a good precaution."

Two weeks later, his wife called me to say, "Eric, I don't know what made you tell my husband to see a pulmonologist. I don't even know if I want to thank you. But he did it."

"Oh?" I said.

"Yes, he has lung cancer. He's undergoing treatments to shrink the tumor before they try to operate. It looks like we have a long, hard road ahead."

How would I handle that situation today, after many more

years of face reading? The professional response would be to stick to the question I was asked; the human response would be to sound the alarm and urge treatment. The best answer I can give is, probably the same way. Given the urgency of the need, I'd count on my human side to help me figure out a way to explain it.

The Face of Death

Face readers don't constantly analyze people. It would be impossible to function if you were bombarded with data on everyone you met. To avoid being overwhelmed, you sort of retract your antennae until you have a reason to do a reading. But some signs are impossible to ignore or miss.

One such sign is the Hippocratic face, a set of facial characteristics that Hippocrates identified around 400 BC. He wrote that if

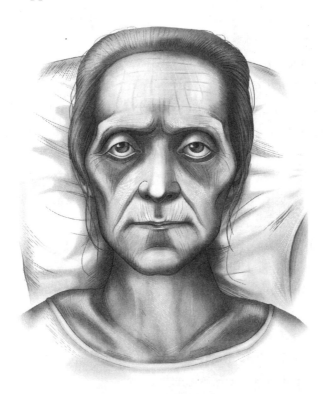

you observe: "the nose sharp; the eyes sunken; the temples fallen in; the ears cold and drawn in and their lobes distorted; the skin of the face hard, stretched and dry; and the colour of the face pale or dusky . . . and if there is no improvement . . . it must be realized that this sign portends death."[1]

The Chinese consider these changes evidence of loss of energy, caused by anything from burnout or the flu to a terminal illness. Of course, not everyone who's dying exhibits these exact changes, and having two or three of them is not evidence of imminent death. But if they arise quickly and in combination with five or six other signs, especially bloodless lips and a grayish tinge between the eyes or around the nose and chin, they are a powerful indicator of the end of life.

In July 2012, when I was working in Thailand, my father was diagnosed with amyotrophic lateral sclerosis (ALS), which is a degenerative disease affecting nerve cells in the brain and spinal cord. Its name comes from the Greek root *myo,* or "related to muscle," and *trophikos,* or "related to nourishment," and thus means "no muscle nourishment." This lack of nourishment causes hardening, or *sclerosis,* on the sides (*lateral*) of the spinal cord, where the nerve cells governing muscles are located. As this happens, the ALS patient loses the ability to speak, move, and breathe. ALS has afflicted such famous people as theoretical physicist and author Stephen Hawking, jazz great Charles Mingus, and baseball player Lou Gehrig, which is why it is also called Lou Gehrig's disease.

After diagnosis, the typical life expectancy of ALS sufferers is one to three years. But that fall, when I came home from Thailand, I was shocked to see how my father had declined. He was in a wheelchair much of the time, but we kept seeing little victories, like the ability to move an arm for a day or two. By October, I was noticing changes in his face. For one thing, it was becoming a mask, incapable of expressions.

My father was a great James Bond fan. In November, when the movie *Skyfall* opened in Karlsruhe, he was very keen to go. So my brother, nephew, and I packed him and his wheelchair into the car and headed for the local multiplex. As I helped him out, I got a close look at his face and was shattered. Virtually all of the signs of energy loss were present. That usually spells death within not weeks but days—usually no more than seventy-two hours.

I told my nephew to wheel my father in, so I could talk to my brother. "Listen," I said, "anything important you want to tell dad, do it tonight or tomorrow. Don't wait."

At first, he couldn't grasp what I was saying. Once I made him understand, we went into the theater, but the movie was a blur. I could barely take my eyes off my father, trying to internalize him, to imprint his image in my brain. After the show, I made light of my need to photograph him and even had the three of us gather around his wheelchair while a stranger snapped group shots. I knew they would be the last pictures we'd ever have.

When I awoke the next morning, I was in tears—not consciously mourning but perhaps starting to process the loss. I went to see my father, who had been sweating all night, my mother said—a final sign. There would be little time to tell him everything that was in my heart, but I showed him my latest book and the text of a talk I had given—partly to get his blessing and make him proud, but even more to remind him that I was capable of assuming the family affairs. Given his strong sense of responsibility, I knew that he would never let go unless he felt confident that someone would take charge and look after my mother.

He died that night. I'd seen the signs of death in people before and have seen them since, but experiencing them up close, with a loved one, gave me a gut-level understanding of their significance. They are not meant to horrify but to advise us. Having a few of the signs tells us, "Your energy, your life-force is under attack."

Having more signs shows that restoring energy is no longer possible. They tell the patient that dying is under way, to accept the process that's unfolding. For the rest of us, they are a powerful warning to find peace, express love, and honor the time that's left.

11

Love

One question I'm asked very often is, "Why do I always fall in love with the wrong person?" The usual reason is that we're attracted to the personality, the innate qualities, but in time the character—which may be deceitful, unkind, or simply dull—shows up.

The person's most communicative features, the eyes and mouth, magnetize us on a subconscious level. No one ever says, "I couldn't resist his chin" or "I fell for her delicate ears." It's always "those gleaming brown eyes" or "those soft lips" that steal hearts. We feel that those eyes shine only for us, which is true. When the other person feels love, it stimulates the hormones that produce the sheen. And when the person smiles and laughs, he or she, with lips parted, is literally opening up to us. We are captivated.

But character, created by outside influences like our culture, our families, and our life experiences, involves a more conscious bond. It requires a meeting of the minds, a sharing of values and expectations. The clash of characters is why seemingly promising relationships go wrong.

When that happens to people a few times, I say, "Don't blame yourself for a losing streak." They're responding to a real subconscious pull, with perhaps too much optimism. But finding a compatible character can be more of a gamble.

I do a lot of joint readings with couples—not necessarily love readings, but ones that let me observe their interactions. As the stories in this chapter show, the way they look at each other, touch each other, and mirror each other's actions reveal the strength of their bond. Sometimes a couple will display distrust—not looking each other in the eye and avoiding each other's touch—which doesn't mean, necessarily, that the relationship is unsalvageable. It's only when respect is gone—they wave off each other's words and turn away from each other, or their microexpressions reveal contempt—that I suspect that it may be time to give up.

What makes people's characters compatible? South American face readers ask, "Do you want a love who's just like you, who fits you perfectly, or do you want the opposite?"

If you choose someone exactly like you, it means that unconsciously you don't expect to learn through the relationship. Whatever growth you experience will have to come from the outside world—a rough-and-tumble job, a challenging environment. You're choosing a relationship that will give you a solid foundation, like a jumping-off place. I'd guess that 60 percent of us choose someone who's the same.

The other 40 percent, who choose their opposites, do expect that their relationships will make them grow—in fact, force them to grow in order to get along. Such people find balance in jobs or other preoccupations that are steady and peaceful.

Relationships can run aground when people's personal and outside lives are too much the same, limiting the opportunities for growth. Too little challenge both at home and in the outside world can prompt people to seek adventure through affairs. (We're often quicker to find fault with a partner than to quit an unstimulating job.) Too many challenges in both places can also spell unhappiness.

Then there's the question of need. People living in a losing way are always needy, and the people they attract or choose when they're in that state may not be the most compatible over time. People who are natural givers may find fulfillment in caring for others, but they must be careful not to lose too much energy. They should be sure to replenish themselves by receiving.

As the stories in this chapter show, love means being in sync with a partner's personality, finding comfort and growth in that person, as well as feeling harmony with the person's character. People whose love endures usually have those two points of connection.

Blue Nails

"How can I find love?" is one of the most common questions I'm asked as a face reader. Often, those asking are attractive, accomplished people who might seem unlikely to have problems with romance. One was an Australian woman, a top executive in her thirties who consulted me in Hong Kong. "I'm a success and I look hot," she told me—and she did, with long, silky blond hair and a gym-toned figure. Funny, I didn't even notice at first. What caught my eye were her blue fingernails.

"So what's wrong with me?" she was saying, "I haven't had more than a few dates in five years."

I've talked about King faces in women, and hers was a classic: strong bone structure, a diminutive mouth with thin lips, eyes with small pupils, and a smile that revealed a vertical line down the center of each cheek. These are lines of command, showing a willingness to fight for dominance. Her jaws were pronounced and muscular. Well-developed jaws can spell high testosterone or high tension, which makes you grind your teeth, or, in some very thin women, bulimia. Whatever the cause, strong jaws mean power—the ability to bite down, crack bone, and devour prey—or at the very least unrelenting determination.

The King traits aren't necessarily negative in either sex, but they can be expressed in a winning or a losing way. Some of the winning qualities are leadership, kindness to the "little people," self-assurance, directness, creativity, and quick thinking. The losing qualities may include being aggressive, stubborn, and driven; overanalytic and unemotional; and addiction- or obsession-prone (drawn to sex, alcohol, and drugs or clinging to rules and routines like working out).

My client's microexpressions put her on the losing side. She rarely smiled but made quick, pointed expressions with her mouth, pushing her lips forward. Her eyes were constantly darting around the room. She seemed to be on high alert, expecting an attack, in warrior mode.

As I studied her face, she scratched her nose. There were those nails again. Colors like blue and black were in fashion, I knew, but I'd never found them so distracting.

She scared men away, I told her. "If you seem aggressive, a man with a weaker personality will think you might bite his head off."

"I don't want a man I can intimidate," she said. "I want an

equal partner. But it's true that in my career, I've had to be a warrior."

"A man as strong as you will be a warrior too," I said. "So he'll be looking for balance, the yin to his yang. He probably doesn't want another battle to fight. You have to lead with your more relaxed and joyful side."

She understood. I explained that, to make a connection, she should stop letting her glance dart around and let a man's eyes rest on hers. Rather than purse her lips to make a point, she should consciously stretch them wider and smile, to seem welcoming. To calm herself, she might relax some of her routines.

"Chinese face readers say, 'The King rules from the throne in the second half of life,'" I told her. "That means he's finally achieved enough to shift his focus from empire building to other realms, like love. You need to pull back a bit from work, to find the energy for romance, as well as the time."

"Okay, I can try," she said. "It might take me a while to shift gears. But is there one simple thing I can do right now that might make a difference?"

"Yes," I said. I had to talk about her nails. A feature that leaps out at you, my masters taught, should never be ignored. "Blue nails on a woman with curly hair, full lips, and big pupils—all the stereotypical feminine characteristics—look artsy and fun. But on a woman with your features, they underscore your King nature, since blue is the color of royalty. They look menacing. Red, pink, or even pearly nails will immediately soften your appearance."

"Oh, come on. I can't believe you read fingernails."

"Everything counts," I said, reflecting on how often a single curious finding can unlock the truth of a situation.

"Well, I doubt that men really notice."

"Isn't it worth a try?" I said. "It's such a minor change."

As she grudgingly agreed, we had to laugh about how hard it can be for a King personality to take advice.

The Homebody

For many people, marriage means companionship to such an extent that they feel uncomfortable functioning alone. That's why friends of one of my clients, a successful art gallery owner and charity-event organizer, couldn't imagine why she attended every opening and gala—and even family holiday gatherings—without her husband. People who'd known her for years hadn't even met him.

She was besieged with questions: Isn't it weird coming to a big event without an escort? Is he incapacitated? Are you two estranged? Doesn't he care about your work? Does he think he's too good for us?

She'd come for a nutrition reading that had branched into a life discussion. She was a pure Jade face, living in an especially winning way. She ticked virtually all the Jade face boxes. She was immersed in beauty, being in the art world, and through her gallery shared her passions with others. She brought her vivid imagination to her charity work and helped create exciting fund-raisers. But Jade faces can be oversensitive to criticism, like the badgering of her friends. They also tend to compromise too much for the sake of peace, which might well be an issue with her husband.

"He's unusual," she said. "He's like a hermit, happy at home, not interested in anything social or even the arts. I gave up trying to drag him to the theater long ago. If I forced him to come to my openings, he'd be a distraction, off by himself, looking bored. I'd rather celebrate my artist and chat up potential buyers than worry about him. People just can't understand that."

"What does he do with himself?" I asked.

"He has a good job and works hard. In his downtime he keeps up with politics and sports—things that don't interest me. He also putters around the house and can fix anything, even the car. He likes working with his hands and solving mechanical problems. We're really opposite types."

"A lot of women would complain, but you seem happy just talking about him."

"I am happy," she said. "He makes me feel like the most vibrant woman in the world. He doesn't want me to stay home and look after him. It doesn't bother him at all when I do things with friends. When I head out, all dressed up for fancy events, he tells me I look beautiful and that he's proud of me. Hearing me describe an evening is more fun for him than being there. And I like the feeling that he's there, a rock-solid foundation, while I flit around. Whatever happens, I know that I can rely on him completely."

"Wow," I said. "I'd love to meet this extraordinary man."

She laughed. "I doubt that you ever will. But here's his picture."

I was fascinated to see that he had a Wall face, a shape more common in Asia than in the West. It's a face wider than it is high. All the qualities she described in her husband—being intractably introverted but reliable and solid, loving facts and practical matters (sports and politics instead of the arts), being goal-oriented and drawn to straightforward mechanical problems (fixing things)—added up to a veritable textbook definition. If I had to describe the worst nightmare of a Wall face, it would be getting stuck in the buffet line, at a huge gala, with his wife's gowned and tuxedoed friends clamoring to meet him. I mention the buffet line because Wall faces like simple paths to a goal—a full stomach—and hate to face complicated choices.

She was right that I'd probably never meet him, because a Wall face would never voluntarily come for a reading. They are strictly pragmatic and rational. One of the life sentences I would give a Wall face would be: *Embrace something that doesn't make sense—you grow by reaching beyond logic.*

This Wall face seemed to have done so by choosing a wife who filled in his gaps: who'd built a life around art, with its abstract pleasures, and dynamic social engagement. Through her he was exposed to realms of life he would never otherwise experience. He, too, was living in a winning way.

The saying "opposites attract" sometimes applies to couples who, down the road, will be torn apart by their differences—or who will stay together only because one partner allows his or her needs to be completely steamrolled by the other. But some find stimulation or a reassuring solidity in an opposite sensibility. They often feel that they're always learning, which makes the relationship that much more fulfilling.

No one can tell us which kind of partner is best for us: someone similar enough to understand and reaffirm who we are or someone whose differences will be challenging but inspiring. Love is a mystery.

The Savior

Sometimes people have powerful bonds that are destined to keep them unhappy. That was the case with a couple from Amsterdam. The wife, who was in her late thirties, often came to my lectures. We'd chat afterward, and she seemed so interested in the process that I expected her to book a reading. But when she finally did, it wasn't for herself but for her husband.

She seemed quite unnerved when she made the appointment, which was puzzling. Was she afraid of what I'd tell him? Or of what he'd tell me?

What struck me when I met him was how contradictory he seemed. He had a classic Tree face, long and wide, with lines forming a U from his mouth to his chin. But his behavior and features were those of a King face. He had a high-profile position at a bank—a King-like job—and, in his fifties, the musculature of a gym addict who worked out every day. His mouth was King-like, with a thick lower lip and a skimpy upper one, as was his beard, well-trimmed, extending from long sideburns, and pointed at the bottom. The sideburns even gave him a resemblance to the man nicknamed the King, Elvis Presley.

A Tree aspiring to be a King—that's not such an unusual combination in a man. But when he spoke, there was another level of complication. His voice was not all King-like, but soft and defensive, emerging from an almost closed, nearly immobile mouth. It was as if he were swallowing his words, reluctant to be heard. That mouth, which looked so stiff and blocked, barely capable of kissing, suggested that his love life was an issue.

When I asked if love was the trouble, he said, "How did you guess?"

After I explained, he told me the story of his marriage. He and his wife had been together for twenty years, since she was in her teens. "Though I left once when I caught her cheating on me. After two years, I came back. I couldn't stay away."

"Wow. Did she regret it?" I asked.

"No, she denied it. I'd hired a detective, who took pictures. But even the evidence couldn't make her admit it. I think she felt too guilty. So I just stopped pressing for the truth."

"Could you forgive her?" I wondered if this was the secret that had her worried. "Are you back to normal married life?"

"Well, if you're asking if we have sex, the answer is no. We never did. We've always slept in separate rooms."

"So why did you get married?"

"Without me, she wouldn't be alive."

When they got together, she'd been a junkie, he said. He'd known her since grade school but lost touch while he was in college. During that time, she fell into the drug scene and got addicted to heroin. Like a typical Tree, he'd wanted to save her. He'd rescued her, literally, from the streets.

"I pushed her into rehab," he told me. "More than once. That relapse cycle was tough on both of us. Finally, she OD'd and wound up in the hospital. That shook her, and with my urging, at last she embraced drug treatment. She'd be the first to tell you I saved her life."

King-like, almost patriarchal. "So she married you. Didn't you have sex then?"

"Not really. I didn't want to shake her equilibrium at first. Then, when she was more stable, she couldn't fulfill my sexual needs."

"Maybe she cheated to see if she could satisfy a man? Or because she needed affection?" By then I felt emboldened to ask such questions. "What was the problem?"

"I need a woman to dominate me in bed. She couldn't manage that. She still can't."

Another layer of crazy contradiction. She'd fallen in love with him for saving her life, a visceral, almost unshakeable connection. In rescuing her, he had behaved as a Tree, and then, when pushing her into rehab, had behaved as a King, even more forceful. How could she handle the fact that, in bed, he was exactly the opposite of the man he was in her life?

In turn, he'd fallen in love with a woman who'd needed him to engineer her very survival. The act of saving her was obviously critical to his identity, an expression of his Tree and King nature. How could he expect the same woman to assume a role in bed that was the polar opposite of why he'd chosen her?

They were stuck, bound together by the rescue, but each expecting something that the other couldn't deliver.

I explained all this, saying, "So how can you live together? Wouldn't you be more fulfilled if you could agree to honor your past but move on?"

"We tried that," he said. "We came back to each other."

At that point, he stopped talking and ended the session. It wasn't my place to argue. I'd rendered my observations and could only hope they'd spark reflection. They were still married when I ran into his wife again a few years later.

Had she been so anxious about the reading because her husband would reveal dark secrets—her infidelity, her addiction? Had she worried that my assessment would empower her husband to leave again? Or was she afraid that I'd somehow validate his wish to stay and thwart her longed-for liberation?

The Coffee Fraud

I often ask clients, "How well do you know yourself?" I'm always shocked when people say, "One hundred percent."

I estimate that I know myself only about 80 percent, so 20 percent of the time I still surprise myself, for better or worse. So how well can you know a partner—even a spouse? I think 50 percent is pretty good when it comes to the unconscious workings of those who share our lives.

But that's still more than any outside figure, like a therapist or a friend (or a face reader). So I always tell clients, "Trust your intuition" once you've determined that it truly derives from knowledge of your partner, not from some disaffection or insecurity within yourself.

When a woman asked me to read a photo of a man, my first

thought was, "Seriously? Are you testing me?" All I could see in the image was a coffee mug and, behind it, a bald scalp and two eyes. "I can see he drinks coffee," I said, glibly.

"I'm sorry," she told me. "It's the only picture I could find. Please, I really need your advice."

I peered closely at the photo. Obviously, in holding the mug, the man was deliberately creating a barrier. I've seen this tactic often in my work with the police—someone who's not telling the truth or who is on guard for some reason will often erect a wall, in any way he can—holding up a pen or a piece of paper, for example. If you're out on a date and your companion lines up the salt and pepper shakers between you, it's not a good sign. Nor is it when your boss flips open a laptop when you've just started discussing a raise. The man's gesture in the photo, blocking his face with a coffee mug, was even more emphatic.

But behind the mug, I could make out some features worth analyzing. The man had four or five thin vertical lines between his eyes, intersected in spots by a few angled horizontal fragments above his brows, in the material zone. This was nothing like the grid pattern of lines that can connote mathematical talent. It was more of a disordered assemblage suggesting unpredictable thinking—maybe aggressive, maybe benign, but definitely not focused and harmonious.

His eyes looked demanding, with tight, hard pupils. Even more telling, I could see a band of white sclera above the iris of his eyes. Visible sclera above the iris signifies negative emotions, like jealousy or rage, as if the weight of the hostility had forced the iris down to the bottom of the eyeball. The man in the picture was angry, maybe just in the moment, but, given the other signs, more likely as a matter of temperament.

One thing I could tell the woman with certainty was, "I wouldn't trust this man."

"That's what I think," she said. "The man is my husband. Everyone thinks I'm crazy—that he's so charming and kind—but lately there's something cold and mean in him."

Oh no! I thought. *Am I blowing up a marriage over a few features behind a mug?*

I started to say, "I should really see his full face before I draw any conclusions. . . ." But she interrupted.

"That's not necessary. I can feel in my bones that something's wrong. All I needed was confirmation that it's reasonable to doubt him."

My validation of her feelings empowered her to confront her husband. They'd only been married for four years, but he admitted that, for the last two, he'd been seeing another woman. Sadly, her intuition (and my conjecture, based on what little I could see) proved accurate. I never heard what finally happened, but the experience underscored an important lesson—as much for me as for my clients: "Trust yourself."

The Choice

We can all recognize sadness in the moment—head bowed, eyes staring into space, evidence of tears—but long-term heartbreak is also reflected in the face. For one thing, the facial muscles aren't as flexible. It takes more than thirty muscles to laugh or give a passionate kiss. That's why kissing and laughing are so healthy.

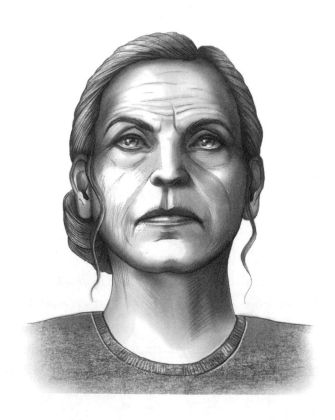

When those muscles go unexercised, their range of movement grows limited.

I noticed that kind of stiffness in the face of a woman who came for a reading. There was a horizontal wrinkle across her philtrum, like a sawhorse blocking a road. Also, from the inside corner of one eye, she had a line stretching across the socket and wending its way down her cheek—piercing "the pillow of power"—like the track of a tear. Both of her eyes were red-tinged and watery.

"I'd like to talk about nutrition," she said. I was stunned. Her skin looked perfectly evenly colored and textured. Though she was in her late forties, she had no dark under-eye circles, puffy eyelids, or sagging jowls. I wanted to say, "Whatever you're eating, keep it up. It's working!"

Biting my tongue, I studied her more closely. I rarely presume to tell clients what kind of reading they should have. If someone wants a Life Purpose consultation, for example, I don't say, "No, let's focus on health," though I'd advise the person to see a doctor about problems I detect. But in this case, the woman's face displayed such clear signs of grief that I had to ask, "Wouldn't you rather talk about love?"

Caught off guard, she burst into tears—great, convulsing sobs, as if she'd suppressed them for decades. As it turned out, she had. All I could do was murmur words of comfort. Finally, the storm passed, and she said, "Thank you. You must have intuited what even I didn't realize—the real reason I came here today."

Some twenty years before, she'd had an intensely passionate affair with a younger man. He was a handsome mechanic, while she was a promising graduate student. Her work attracted the attention of a professor ten years older, who was charming and accomplished. When he asked her out, she accepted, flattered, though their physical bond proved to be "just okay."

For a while, she dated both of them. "But I couldn't take it," she told me. "I was at an age when it was time to settle down. So I had to decide—to stay with the mechanic, who felt like the love of my life, or to marry the professor, who was intellectually compatible, respectable, and kind."

She made the safe choice. Within months, she was pregnant, but before her son was born, the professor was diagnosed with multiple sclerosis. He was soon bedridden, so she abandoned her academic career to support her family as a speech therapist. "My son, who's sixteen, is my pride and joy," she said, "but it was hard to raise him alone. My husband, who's completely paralyzed, is another challenge."

She was resigned to her life, but then one day, on the street, she bumped into the mechanic.

They laughed and cried with joy at rediscovering each other. For the next few hours, they sat in a café, comparing notes on their lives. He too was married, with three children he adored, though he and his wife had drifted apart. As they said good-bye, they exchanged phone numbers.

That night, she got a text. "I still love you," he wrote.

She answered, "I love you. I always did."

I realized that I was holding my breath, fearing the questions, "What should I do? Should I ask him to leave his wife and kids? Should I abandon my husband? Can we reset the clock on our love?"

Luckily, she didn't ask. Instead, she said, "Thank you for listening. There's never been anyone I could share this with—not my friends and certainly not my son. I'm so grateful that you recognized my heartbreak and let me express it. Just confiding my story has been a profound relief."

Anatomy of Connection

I'm frequently consulted about relationship problems, both active turbulence and the more subtle sense of estrangement or growing apart. For couples who want to stay together, it's worth trying one or more of the following physical strategies, which can help refresh your bond:

- Look into each other's eyes. By this, I mean sit face-to-face in a quiet place, away from all distractions, and stare straight into the eyes of your partner. You don't have to touch, but resist the urge to laugh (it's okay to smile) or mentally check out. Hold your partner's gaze as long as you can—for three minutes at first, then work up to five or more minutes—the longer, the better. This exercise releases, in each of you, the powerful hormone oxytocin, which promotes bonding. I encourage couples to perform it once a week.
- Touch in passing. Whenever you're near each other, be sure to touch. You don't have to grab each other or hold hands or otherwise be dramatic about it, but simply touch for a moment. This creates a sensual link between you.
- Twice a day—when you go to bed and when you rise—smell your partner's forehead close to the hairline. His or her unique smell, created by hormones, sweat, and so on, emanates from this spot. If you love someone, this smell can grow addictive. If you don't, it may become repellent.

These strategies obviously can't overcome serious differences, which you may need therapy to solve, but they can reaffirm the visceral connection that makes a solution worth seeking.

One of our strongest affirmations of connection is, of course, a kiss. Where and how we kiss conveys meaning to face readers.

- A kiss on the forehead, for face readers, is the highest expression of love. The forehead is the bony plate protecting your brain, the site of all thoughts and emotions. It's also topped by the hairline, where you can smell the essence of the person. Kissing someone on the forehead—or leaning in to touch foreheads—is a direct embrace of the person's body and soul. The elevated passion of such a kiss is hard to fake.
- The mouth is the most common place to kiss, though in a way it doesn't make sense to plant your lips on the opening to a person's digestive system. In Chinese tradition, a kiss on the mouth signifies lust. It can also mean love, of course—the mouth is the site of communication—but think about how often people exchange mouth kisses with those they don't even like.
- Kissing on the eyelids is an occasional gesture, not something people do every day. It may signify a wish to be even closer to the person than kissing the forehead, since the eyes are the window to the soul.

Passion

In the Middle East, I met a woman in her twenties who, as is customary there, was still living at home. Her boyfriend, who'd just proposed marriage, was an older, newly divorced man with two children and a high-level job that kept him hopping between continents. Eager to leave home and launch her own life, she was thrilled to have found a man with whom she had (in her words) a strong spiritual connection. They seemed compatible, according to the separate Life Purpose reading I did for each of them. But then they asked for a joint relationship reading to gain perspective on their engagement.

Watching them sit side by side and interact, I grew disheartened. Each had spoken of their joy in the relationship—telling me how lucky they'd felt to find each other—but caution signs were flashing in my head. I hated to say, "I'm sorry. I know that you share a lot of interests, but I don't see bright prospects for your marriage."

They were shocked. The man felt insulted and even questioned my abilities. "Nothing is a hundred percent," I said, "including the validity of my opinion. But if you want a reading, all I can do is tell the truth. It's up to you whether or not you accept it."

"Okay, tell us," they insisted.

Their face shapes were the first thing I mentioned. The man, not surprisingly for a businessman, had a King face, with strong jaws, prominent cheekbones, and smallish eyes. The woman was a typical Fire face, with a wide forehead, pointed chin, and an eagerness to please. But neither was engaging productively, given their microexpressions.

I told the man, "When I focus on your girlfriend, you pull up one corner of your mouth, narrow your eyes, and glance back and forth between us. You look angry and possessive, like you're jealous."

"He's jealous, all right," the woman said. "Just now, on our way over, he fumed because he thought the cabbie was staring at me in the rearview mirror. Yesterday, in a restaurant, he got mad when I said two words to the handsome waiter. He even hates it when I'm giggling with my girlfriends."

The man sighed and admitted, "I guess I am jealous. I don't know why. I've never felt this way before, not even with my ex-wife."

His fiancée laughed. But then I said, "You're not that secure either. The way you stare at his mouth implies that you're hoping for a hint of intimacy, of reassurance. I bet you're suspicious and always checking up on him."

Now the man laughed. "Oh yeah. When I put down my smartphone, she's all over it. If she sees my wife's number, she has to know every detail: What did she say? What did she want?"

The Fire face's challenge is to overcome self-doubt and chronic mistrust. Having always lived at home, the woman hadn't yet learned to trust herself, never mind trust a man in his forties with family obligations who was always on the road. As for her fiancé, being a King, he had to resist aggression and the urge to dominate others. Rather than connecting in a winning way, they were each bringing out the other's losing qualities.

The way they looked at each other held another major clue. People tend to affirm bonds of affection with what's called the "triangle gaze." Rather than stare straight into the other person's eyes, they tend to look at one eye, then down to the mouth, then up to the other eye, quickly and unconsciously. The recipient of the triangle gaze might mirror it or might respond by raising the eyebrows slightly and parting or otherwise stimulating the lips. These movements arouse the hormones of connection.

But this man looked from one eye down to the woman's upper chest before returning his gaze to her other eye. That look conveys lust rather than love—not because he's checking out her bustline, though some men do that, but because he's skipping the mouth, the portal of communication. He's more beholding her than bonding with her. Her response—staring at his mouth—suggested her anxious desire to connect with him.

"I understand your attraction." I told them, explaining these signs. "I can see how your personalities could mesh. But the bond that connects you is less true love than a kind of passion, for which the German word is *leidenschaft*. It means 'creating pain.'"

The man asked an interesting question. "So to become more

bonded—what if we started over in another city, like London, where my firm has an office, away from the distraction of my family and her friends? Would that help?"

"I can't predict that," I had to say. "But you'd still have to travel, so living in a strange place might make her even more insecure, and there would be plenty of men in London to make you jealous."

I stressed that I couldn't tell them what to do because, in my role as a Messenger, I can only describe what I see. I reiterated that I couldn't guarantee that I was right—that it was up to them to examine their relationship and decide if and how they could improve it. They left looking thoughtful and a little dejected.

Some months later, I heard from both of them, separately. They'd split up, the woman told me, because of his jealousy. "He kept telling me how to act. I felt like a little kid." The man had a different take: he'd realized that, in the vulnerability and confusion of divorce, he wasn't ready to jump into marriage.

Neither regretted the breakup, it seemed, since they both thanked me. As the man said, "Just hearing you describe our problems out loud was therapeutic."

Rekindling

The triangle gaze was a major factor in a reading I did with a couple in New York. In the past, they'd booked individual nutrition readings, but they now wanted to look at their relationship. Often I do relationship readings with one member of a couple, using a photo of the other. But since I knew them both, I recommended a joint reading, which might offer deeper insight.

"Okay," the wife said. "But you should know that we're getting a divorce."

That jolted me. The revelation was so dramatic, for one thing;

for another, I had to wonder what people who were splitting up hoped to gain from a reading.

"How long have you been together?" I asked.

"More than twenty years," she told me. "We've been married for the last ten."

I expected her to do most of the talking because she had a Dragon face, combining King, Jade, and Fire qualities. In Chinese mythology, the Dragon is a very powerful personality. People with Dragon faces are usually problem solvers and tend to dominate in their relationships. The husband had a typical Tree face, suggesting that he was a loner, since a tree is protected by bark. Like a Tree, he looked rooted sitting across from me, lost in his thoughts.

"Is there a reason that this is happening now?" I said. "Addiction? Infidelity? A major argument?"

"Oh no. Nothing like that." The wife was sitting beside her husband, almost but not quite touching, and as she spoke they kept exchanging glances.

"We're like roommates," she said. "Comfortable, companionable. But it's been years since we've connected on any intimate level. We just talk about the day-to-day stuff, like, 'Did you buy milk?' or 'Have you seen my umbrella?' We don't have kids to keep us together. It's like we've lost interest in each other."

Between their eyebrows, they both had deep, parallel vertical lines that marked them as strong, pragmatic thinkers. That made me suspect that they'd reached an intellectual, rather than heart-driven, decision to part. Before and after she spoke, the wife checked in with him visually, and as he listened to her, his face softened. Clearly, the two cherished each other.

"I think you're crazy to break up," I said. "You're so natural together that you anticipate each other's gestures. You seem so totally in sync. I think it would be hard for either of you ever to find such a perfect partner."

"But we never even have sex," the wife said.

"That can feel wounding," I said to both of them. "It can make you feel estranged."

I told them about the triangle gaze and how often I observed it in their interactions. "That means you're not psychically estranged. You're constantly shoring up your bond. Even to an outsider you have a perceptible—clearly sensual—connection. There must be some embers you can fan into flame, to learn to have sex again."

I said to the husband, "You're a Tree, so you can be inflexible and passive. Instead of making an effort, you tend to wait out problems, hoping they'll go away. Now it's time either to act yourself or else plan to follow your wife's lead."

I told the wife, "You're the Dragon, the problem solver. It may be up to you to initiate change. That Tree is loyal and devoted.

He's probably too earthbound to come up with ideas. But he can respond if you shake his branches."

They laughed at that image, leaning a little closer together. "You might not have sex the way you did in your twenties," I said, "even if our culture claims that you can, or that you should. But just having sex isn't the goal as much as refreshing your relationship. If you've lost interest in each other, create the vibrancy to rediscover it. Give yourself a new backdrop for interaction— take an exotic trip, or a class. It's worth reinvesting in a love like yours before you decide to split. Besides," I told the wife, "Dragons don't give up so easily. They are persistent."

The wife stroked her husband's arm, then reached down and took his hand. He clutched it like a precious gift, with a smile on his face. As they left, they looked deeply relieved, as if the heavy burden of their own expectations of themselves had been lifted.

12

Perception

How are we perceived? Once we begin looking consciously at others, recognizing that we have a constant, wordless exchange of information, it's natural to wonder how they see us. It can even be possible to influence their impressions. As this chapter shows, every clue counts when evaluating a person.

We discussed communicative clues, like gestures and facial expressions, in chapter 7, "The World of Expression." But there are also unintended clues that can teach us about a person.

The way the person walks, for example. In Asia, especially, a lot of women walk a bit knock-kneed, with their thighs close together and feet farther apart. This signifies lack of confidence, being withdrawn and unwilling to draw attention. An ordinary gait, with legs parallel, doesn't convey much, and nor does a wide-legged stride in a heavyset person, who is probably trying to maintain balance. But in a person of average size, walking wide-legged announces, "Here I am! Give me space! I'm in charge!" If I were reviewing such a person for a leadership role, I would welcome such a stride. But in a less elevated job, I'd wonder if that person might feel stifled.

Handedness is another important clue. Only 10 to 15 percent of the global population is left-handed, but the percentage is much higher among superachievers. Half of the U.S. presidents since World War II have been lefties: Harry Truman, Gerald Ford, Ronald Reagan (ambidextrous or mixed-handed), George H. W. Bush, Bill Clinton, and Barack Obama. Other famous left-handers include Steve Jobs, Bill Gates, Mark Zuckerberg, Oprah Winfrey, and Ruth Bader Ginsberg (women are statistically less likely to be left-handed than men), as well as many musicians, including Paul McCartney, Ringo Starr, David Bowie, Kurt Cobain, and Lady Gaga. In some sports, left-handers have an edge, so it's not surprising that many of the greats from baseball's Babe Ruth to tennis champions John McEnroe, Jimmy Connors, and Monica Seles are lefties.

Not all left-handed people are successful, of course. They're also well represented at the bottom of the achievement spectrum and are more prone to certain physical and mental health problems. But there is a lot of evidence that they do think differently. They process information more quickly and, rather than attack problems with left-brain logic, often come up with novel, intuitive solutions. They can be visionary and inspiring.

The stories below offer a few more observations that we can factor in to our assessments of people, and that they in turn may unconsciously pick up about us.

Personal Style

Whether we're male or female, hair is like a banner proclaiming our identity to the world. The way we wear it is intensely personal, to a degree that I almost didn't understand myself. I'm fairly casual about my appearance, but I got a jolt one day while working in Hawaii, when, desperate for a haircut, I dropped in to the fancy hotel salon. The stylist, who would sneer at the term "barber," parted my hair on the right and started snipping. I thought he was just cutting until I realized that he was creating a capital-letters STYLE: leaving my hair parted on the wrong side, swept completely off my forehead, and gelled into place.

"It looks good," he said.

"It might on someone else, but not on me."

We got into a philosophical discussion about haircuts, with me insisting that a style wasn't "good" unless it fit the client's personality. "A haircut means something," I said. " It plays a huge role in how we're perceived." The stylist somewhat agreed but challenged me to prove I was right: to "perceive" the nature of the next client who walked in by his hair alone, without considering other features like eyes, mouth, and face shape.

I was a bit nervous at first. Usually, hair is an add-on to refine what we see in the primary features. But I got lucky with the next client, who had a beard, a great source of insight, and hair that was especially revealing.

The guy was in his late twenties, with brown, collar-length hair parted down the middle, flyaway on the top and sides and curly at the ends. The center part suggested perfectionism, which was contradicted by the tousled, longish curls, a typical indicator of romance, sensitivity, and idealism. His forehead came to a point at his hairline, also a sign of creativity and depth.

His eyebrows were mismatched, with a solid brow on the right and a broken one on the left, where a short tuft appeared on the inside corner, split off from the brow itself. A tuft set apart that way implies a rift between the guy and his culture or family of origin. The fact that it appeared on the left (governed by the right, feeling, imaginative side of the brain) implied that he was cut off from or unsupported by the people most connected to his emotions.

His beard was short but shaggy and uneven, bushier on the right side than on the left. It was also patchy, with hairless areas below his lips. His untrimmed mustache, drooping over his lips in places, had a lot of hairs sticking straight out. The untamed mustache implied a reluctance to share feelings, and the thinness and spottiness of his beard signaled that he was easily hurt.

His generally unkempt air made me see him as a rebel, one who didn't give much thought to his appearance or behavior. It suggested that, while he was warmhearted, he had potential to go to extremes in melancholy or temper. In some face-reading traditions, the scruffy beard would indicate that he was meant to lead but would be defeated by being out of balance.

When I gave the young man my analysis, he was stunned. "So much of what you say is accurate," he told me. Then he laughed. "I guess I'd better get a beard trim as well as a haircut."

I completely won over the stylist. "Okay," he said, "you made your point. The fact that you could read all that from a guy's hair gives me a new perspective on my mission. It's about more than grooming and fashion. You've shown me how completely a hair style can affect our estimation of a person."

The Man in the Mirror I

A CEO client was anxious about some contract negotiations. "I hate dealing with these guys," he told me. "They bombard me with information, and they all talk at once. Then they push me to respond, so I lose focus and make mistakes. Come along to the meeting and help me."

I agreed to accompany him with the caveat that I wasn't sure what I could do. The meeting began with a multiple martini lunch. The presentations afterward were animated, with a lot of crosstalk. When I got a kick under the table, I knew that the CEO was saying, "Help! I'm getting lost in all the chatter."

So I began to yawn, subtly at first, but then more visibly, every few minutes, without covering my mouth. One by one, the guys talking began to flag. It wasn't long before one of them said, "Let's table this and pick it up tomorrow." My client agreed, overjoyed. The break gave him the chance to process the discussion and to figure out his strategy.

We've all observed that yawning is contagious, but the reason has long been unknown. In the 1990s, a team of Italian neuroscientists headed by Giacomo Rizzolatti discovered a compelling explanation: the very same neurons in macaque monkeys' brains fired when they grabbed a peanut and when they watched another monkey grab one. The scientists called these brain cells "mirror neurons."[1]

Research in humans demonstrated similar effects. A study led by Marco Iacoboni at UCLA showed that mirror neurons might echo not just actions but also intentions. A person picking up a teacup to drink from it activated neurons different from those of a person picking up a teacup to clear the table. So when a person yawns, it's likely that someone watching might unconsciously copy not just the action but also the yawner's mood—fatigue, boredom, or distraction.[2]

Scientists remain divided over how mirror neurons work, whether there are different mirror systems governing actions and emotions, and even whether they actually exist. Many think that they evolved to help us quickly share knowledge. As brain imaging grows more sophisticated, research shows they may underlie important human functions, including self-awareness and, especially, empathy.

The Man in the Mirror II

I encouraged a different client, a businessman from Geneva, to employ the empathy function of mirror neurons in negotiations. He'd actually come for a crash course in face reading to apply to his work. Over five or six sessions, he'd gotten quite proficient at detecting face shapes and the broad strokes of personalities. But microexpressions, which can be the key to understanding, are more subtle and hard to assess.

One day he called long-distance in frustration. He was engaged in a tough transaction. "I just can't tell if I'm making headway," he complained. "The lawyer I'm dealing with hardly says a word."

"Watch his face closely," I told him. "Make a point of remembering his expressions. Then excuse yourself, go into the restroom, and imitate those expressions in the mirror."

Later, the businessman called to report. "Well, I did what you said, and I had an *aha!* moment. It struck me that he was waiting for one more concession—to feel that he'd 'won.' So I threw in an easy one. That clinched it."

This method is not foolproof, of course, but by copying a person's expressions, often you can re-create his state of mind within yourself. Stimulated by your facial muscles, mirror neurons can help your brain conjure another person's emotions and expectations. It's not mind reading, but it's probably as close to it as most of us can get.

You can also bond with a person more effectively by mirroring his facial expressions. We tend to do this unconsciously. That's often why stroke victims feel isolated: because they can't form expressions for people to reflect back, affirming connection. Not surprisingly, there's autism research focused on mirror neurons because they provide social and emotional cues that autistic people often miss. And, as I mentioned, while I'm not opposed to Botox, facial plastic surgery, and the like, it's good to be aware that if they're extreme enough to severely limit microexpressions, they can make it harder to empathize with others and vice versa.

When I give talks, I don't just speak. I use lots of expressions—smiling, squinting, frowning, and so on. I have an animated personality, so that comes naturally to me, but it also really connects me with my audience. It stimulates them to replicate my expressions and thus embrace my ideas. There's a popular comedian, Sebastian Maniscalco, who has very flexible facial muscles and makes wild faces that fire up the crowd and, probably as much as his jokes, make them howl with laughter.

To bond consciously—say, with a stone-faced person—try making an unusual expression. This tactic works especially well with one-sided actions, like winking or raising an eyebrow. The unexpected message will stimulate the other person's mirror neurons, which will try to copy it to determine what you mean. Not only will the person find it hard to stay impassive, but the facial cue will seem less pressuring and intrusive than a verbal plea like, "Talk to me!" or "Tell me what you're thinking!" You may still have to get to words, but you'll have built a bridge to conversation.

The Man on the Phone

One Middle Eastern spa where I worked was part of a luxury hotel chain. When the head of the chain saw face reading listed as a guest service, he asked the spa manager, "What the hell is that?" After hearing a description, he was still unconvinced but curious. So the spa manager asked me to read the guy, but warned, "Be careful! Since he's our boss, he won't want us to see his weaknesses. Don't bring up his character or his health."

"Okay. What about love?" I asked.

"Not that!" the manager said. "Think of something else. I know you can."

So that's what I was contemplating as I waited in my office overlooking the parking area. The big boss was late, but I could see him through my window, talking on his cell phone. Twenty minutes passed, then half an hour. By the time he came inside and apologized for being late, I knew exactly what to tell him. "I understand. It can be hard to break away from talking to your wife."

"How did you know who I was talking to?" He was stunned.

"It was clear from your face and your behavior on the phone," I said. "First of all, your gaze was directed downward the whole time. Looking toward the ground indicates that you're talking about earthly, domestic issues. How are the kids, call grandma, don't forget the milk—the things you discuss with those closest to you. You're wearing a wedding ring, so I surmised it was your wife."

"Incredible," he said. "But I'm also close to my business partner. What if I'd been talking to him about a deal?"

"Then you'd be staring off into space. Your partner might be close to you, but the subject would be less immediate. It wouldn't be so related to an established, material element in your life. Even if you were talking about money, it would be more abstract. You'd be envisioning an idea or an outcome, looking into the future."

The boss smirked a little with his next question. "Now suppose—not that this would ever apply to me—that I was talking to my mistress? Could you tell?"

"Almost certainly," I told him. "You'd be looking downward but with your gaze off to the side, over your shoulder. You'd circle your body inward, as if to hide your face and the phone. Even if I couldn't see the look on your face—affection or anticipation—it would be obvious."

"I'll definitely remember that," he said, with a laugh. Marital fidelity was not his virtue. But his example shows that the way you position your face and direct your gaze can be as revealing about who you are as your features.

The Poker Face

Can you ever completely hide your thoughts?

That's what a couple of professional card players in Macau wanted to know. They hired me to help them gain an advantage at poker tables. "Well, you can create an impenetrable stone face," I told them. "Just keep your face completely still and your gaze blank. Don't move a muscle."

But that wouldn't help them in poker, I explained. The word

impassive, meaning "expressionless" or "unreadable," is more apt than it sounds because keeping a stone face is not really a passive act. It requires distracting concentration. More importantly, moving the muscles in your face stimulates your brain, so if your face is inactive, your brain isn't counting cards, planning your best move, or guessing your opponents' holdings.

So, rather than keep still, it's better to look over your cards, check out the room, size up your competition, and so on—to keep the circuits firing.

"But if we study the other players, they'll sense it," one of them said. "It will seem too obvious."

"But they're expecting you to study them," I said. "You won't be giving them information they don't know. Focusing on them can stop you from revealing thoughts about your own cards as effectively as a classic poker face. Meanwhile, it will keep your brain awake and calculating."

"So you basically hide one thought with another thought!"

"Yes, that's how it works," I said. I offered them more concrete help by teaching them face-reading "tells" that could tip them off to their opponents' cards. We spent a weekend on these lessons, which are too involved to recount. But the big takeaway—the more you read another person, the harder it is for them to read you—is the most useful when it comes to keeping your thoughts to yourself.

The Five-Second Rule

As I've mentioned, when I do a hiring consult, I pay close attention to everything the applicant does. Ideally, I meet the person in the lobby so I can observe elevator behavior. In one case, when I greeted a would-be female manager downstairs, she looked perfectly cool and poised. She introduced herself in a sure, steady

Interruption

We all know monologists, long-winded people who barely pause for breath. They never give us a chance to get a word in edgewise. Rather than snap, "Get to the point!" try these strategies to signal the desire to speak:

- Pucker your lips, bringing them to a point a few times, like a fish. This motion sends the speaker a very strong subconscious signal to stop talking.
- Tug on one of your earlobes to convey, "I want to be heard." This cue is more subtle and may be easier to miss because it doesn't involve the middle of the face.
- Poke your tongue into your cheek, the "pillow of power," to make a visible bump. That tells the speaker that your tongue is trying to break free and talk.

Sometimes a long-winded speaker embroiders a story so much that you have trouble following or believing what's being said. Rolling your eyes, like saying, "Get to the point," signifies total dismissal and is likely to offend. Instead, try the following sequence of steps:

1. Open your eyes wide, to signal surprise at the story.
2. Then briefly cast your gaze upward, as if searching your mind for a way to accept it.
3. Finally, when you look back at the speaker, blink a couple times.

Keep your mouth closed throughout the process to give the speaker the sense that you're digesting the story rather than gearing up to protest it.

The speaker's mirror neurons will re-create the movement, echoing your confusion or disbelief. The closing blinks imply that you don't buy the story. So the speaker, having internalized your doubt, will work to clarify or simplify the story to make it credible.

I often use this technique on law enforcement consults, to challenge the accounts of the accused. If I said, "I don't believe you," a suspect would fight against my opinion. But feeling my doubts in his own mind will push him to come up with a better explanation. That's usually the point where a guilty suspect goes wrong by offering enough contradictory information to look culpable.

voice. As we entered the elevator, her face remained composed and pleasant.

That told me that she was scared to death, even before nervous gestures gave her away—clutching her attaché case to her chest, pressing the elevator button with a pen. Upstairs, as we headed for the conference room, she walked a little knock-kneed, as if fighting for control. Then, when a cup of coffee was placed in front of her, she lifted it by curling her forefinger through the handle, supported by her middle finger's knuckle. She supported the cup from the bottom with her free hand—another telltale sign of anxiety.

Someone who lifts a cup this way tends to like structure and to follow rules. A variant of the finger-through-the-hole method, with a thumb pressed on top of the handle, indicates a person also favors structure but wants to be the boss. The person who wraps fingers around the bowl of a cup, with one finger slipped through the handle, is self-comforting, trying to get centered. The free spirit grabs the rim of the cup with three or four fingers and, risking a spill, guides it to his or her mouth.

The candidate exhibited other signs of fear during the interview, but for me the strongest evidence was the eerie calm she never lost from the moment we met. It violated the Five-Second Rule. There are five-second (or three-second) rules for many situations, including the famous belief that food dropped on the floor and left for just a few seconds is safe to eat. But in face reading, the rule applies to the length of time a person holds a fixed expression. If it's more than five seconds, the expression is fake, a mask hiding feelings. The minute the job candidate kept her composed façade was the equivalent of shouting, "I'm so nervous."

The Five-Second Rule is also a good gauge of whether a person is using his or her face to manipulate us. Children often use this tactic. They're hardwired to study and mimic adults from the moment of birth, so they quickly grasp the nuances of facial expressions. In their preverbal years, they communicate with adults via chatter and cries, using their facial expressions to convey what these vocalizations mean.

So it's common to see a child adopt an expression like a pout, with eyes squinched and lower lip poked out—even trembling—in order to get attention. Of course, a pout followed by bursting into tears may be a sign of genuine frustration, but often a child will hold a pout, glancing from side to side, until the face is spotted by an adult. If a child pouts for more than five seconds—say, in the supermarket, near the candy bars—the face may be less a genuine expression than a clever calculated effort.

The Look of Love

In Switzerland, I had a consult with a vivacious young woman who'd brought in two photographs. "I guess I have a good problem," she said. "For months, I've been dating these two great guys, and now I really have to make a choice."

When she showed me the pictures, I was surprised. Both were extraordinarily attractive—like actor or model handsome—but they were completely different types. One was dark-haired with Mediterranean coloring, while the other looked practically Scandinavian, with almost white-blond hair and light eyes. Had they looked similar, it would have been easier to evaluate them by just focusing on small differences. To make matters worse, both photos were fairly generic—posed headshots that looked as if they'd been taken for a company website, rather than more revealing candid snaps.

"This is a tough call," I had to say. "It's like you're heading in two different directions at once. Are you looking for someone very much like you, or someone who's the opposite?"

"I don't know," she said. "I want the one who's best for me, in an ideal world."

"I wish we lived in an ideal world. All I can do is sum up their pros and cons. You'll have to decide which one appeals the most."

I started listing their strong points, based on face shapes, features, and visible lines. That sparked a debate on the merits of being with a protective King face versus a vibrant Fire face and so on, until I got exasperated. "From these staged photos, I can't see much evidence that either man is living in a losing way," I said. "Since I have no idea how they treat you, they both seem fine. There has to be a better way to tell the difference."

Then it struck me. "Do me a favor. You take each photo and study it closely for a full minute. I'll take notes and tell you what your face shows."

I put the pictures facedown on the table and shuffled them around, so she could make a random choice. "Don't tell me which one you're looking at."

As she studied the first photo, her smile stretched wide and her lips parted. She looked happy and welcoming. But after a few long seconds, she squeezed her eyebrows together and pulled her lips into more of a kissing shape—the face of sympathy and concern. Her gaze softened and grew almost motherly, as if she saw some pain inside and was comforting him. That empathy was probably how they connected to begin with.

"Next picture," I said.

Again, her face lit up at the sight. When she relaxed her smile, her eyes grew dreamy and lifted, half-lidded, to stare off in the distance. As her gaze returned to the image, she looked wistful and absorbed by it.

Now I had my answer, but the choice was hers. "Here's what I see," I told her. "You care deeply for both of them. When you look at photo 1, you grow warm and protective, like you want to wrap the guy in a cocoon of love and heal him. For the guy in photo 2, you're filled with longing, which is not the same as lust. Lust sparks and fades. Longing is more a desire to be enveloped by the person. When you look away from his image and into space, you're projecting your longing into the future. So you have different kinds of love. The question is, which kind do you want?"

She quickly recognized the truth in my assessment. "I want to feel longing for the rest of my life," she said. "I want to desire and be desired. I want to be enveloped. That's what I choose. But the kind of love I have for photo 1 is valid, too. I want to offer him my caring friendship, if he'll accept it. But I see now that my love can't dry his tears."

The Enlightened Face

In chapter 1, "Our First Language," we talked about the many studies that have been done to determine what people consider the "perfect" face. Usually, stories about this research appear in the tabloid press accompanied by photos of whichever young, generically featured star is hot at the moment. No face with interesting quirks ever fits the studies' consensus-based criteria of "perfection."

When I asked my students who they think has the perfect face—which I define not as generic but as "enlightened," or revealing of humanity's best qualities—at least a third of them will say "the Buddha." That's an easy guess because the Buddha is practically the symbol of enlightenment. But Buddhas have many different faces—some laughing, some serene, some in active meditation, some with closed eyes, some with lowered eyes, some with gazing eyes, and so on. It would be difficult to choose just one. The image of the Buddha inspires millions of people, but it's more of a spiritual icon, radiating wisdom, than a human face.

A wise face connotes authority, which can seem unapproachable. That's why my perfect face, along with wisdom, projects a childlike quality of openness—no aggression, no hatred, no detectable inner torment. Being childlike also implies playfulness, a sense of joy that attracts others who want to be uplifted. My perfect face is that of Nelson Mandela (1918–2013).

He has a Bucket face, with deep wrinkles running from the outer edges of his nose to below his chin. It's not necessary to have a Bucket face to serve humanity, but it's the shape of a pragmatic creator, one who can effect realistic change, the shape of a visionary who can motivate and strengthen the resolve of followers.

His forehead is broad, signifying openness and tolerance, and prominent, suggesting a big brain. The two deep wrinkles stretching across it show, on the left, the strength of his intuition, and, on the right, the power of his instincts. His slight widow's peak implies independence but willingness to help and protect others. Even his ears are well oriented, sticking out just enough to show active thinking and being positioned close enough to the head to indicate peacefulness.

He has the eyes of a dreamer, with deep crow's-feet at the

corners, indicating laughter. His microexpression reveals no hint of rage or recrimination, even after a lifetime of oppression and imprisonment for nearly thirty years. His gaze remains steady and compelling. His eyes shine with vibrant imagination and the embrace of life.

His mouth is wide and well shaped and has upturned corners, suggesting a curious, cheerful, and energetic nature, with an inclination toward joy and not a hint of bitterness. His gums show when he smiles—the mark of a giver. His upper and lower lips have the same size and depth, implying a balance between idealism and materialism. Someone with a more materialistic nature, reflected by a prominent lower lip, would not be so idealistic, and a pure idealist would be adrift in his own world. He has the mouth of a leader—welcoming, communicative, and inspiring but also trustworthy and grounded.

Taken together, these features add up to an Enlightened face: wise yet childlike, determined yet open, righteous yet peaceful and joyful. Looking at his visage, you can almost hear him deliver his famous saying, "Tread softly, breathe peacefully, laugh hysterically."

What impression would someone form looking at your face or mine? I can't think of a better wish than for all of us to project our own version of enlightenment.

PART III

A Face-Reading Reference Guide

The Basics of Face Reading

I began this book by saying that we are all face readers. Every single day, we unconsciously use this intuitive power to size up the people we meet, divine their intentions, and ascertain the truths and expectations behind their words. I hope the stories I've told have empowered you to deepen your insights and grow to trust your intuition even more.

Obviously, years of apprenticeship and study can't be compressed into a few—or even many—pages. But in this section, I want to offer some broad strokes of formal face-reading insight, just for easy reference.

To start, in my philosophy and discipline of face reading, there are three guiding principles. I tell my students that failing to observe them will undermine any reading.

1. ***Depict, Don't Predict.*** Face reading is not psychotherapy or fortune-telling. It is the art and science of observation, of assessing elements of the human visage detectable *in the present moment*. We're not studying the face to read the past, as a therapist might. It's not

that someone has an experience like a trauma that shows up as a clear sign—like "X marks the spot"—in his face.

Instead, an experienced face reader judges what the face is saying right now. Perhaps there will be an irregularity suggesting some past event that's worth asking about because it informs the present. But a deep exploration of the client's history to resolve conflicts or neuroses is not our goal. We look for a person's innate strengths and gifts, as well as the potential these traits might suggest.

But judging potential—the way a person might express talents and strengths—is not the same as looking into a crystal ball. We might surmise that a person is living in a winning or losing way—meaning, using his or her gifts in a satisfying or sabotaging way—and explore the effects with that person. But since most people flop back and forth between winning and losing patterns, it's not appropriate to judge what we see as good or bad or try to extrapolate from our observations to make predictions.

2. *Look at Both Sides*. Every face has two sides that represent different qualities, so they can never be perfectly symmetrical. The right side (governed by the left side of the brain) reflects consciousness, logic, and the material world. The left (governed by the right side of the brain) is the side of the subconscious, of idealism, creativity, and dreams. To evaluate a person, you might start by looking at the whole face, but then you must examine each side separately. (Note: the right side of the person facing you is your left side, and vice versa.)

3. *The Eyes and Mouth Are Critical*. There's a reason that the universal representation of a face—the configuration that babies recognize from their first moment of life—is like a smiley emoticon, a circle with two eyes and a mouth. The eyes and mouth are the most flexible features of the face, so they are the most able to communicate. Though the other elements of the face convey important information, the eyes and mouth have special significance.

With these rules in mind, we can consider the properties of faces. Normally, with students, I begin with intensive focus on the all-important eyes and mouth. But as a general introduction to the process—and since we've referenced them so often in the stories—let's start with face shapes.

I. Face Shapes

Face shapes might seem like the easiest face-reading concept to grasp, but in fact they offer merely an outline of the personality—and not a definitive one at that. First of all, the categories of faces were established thousands of years ago for a fairly homogeneous population. Over tens of centuries, we've become much more mobile and more likely to reflect mixtures of influences. Second, our world has grown more complicated over time. Look at the changes we've seen in just the past couple hundred years, spanning both the Industrial Revolution and the Information Age. These changes have certainly altered our sense of time and have likely colored the character of our emotions. It stands to reason that humans would change, too, evolving to keep in step.

No face shape is better or worse to have than any other. Each is associated with potential strengths and weaknesses. When we express our personalities—determined by all our inborn characteristics, including face shapes—in a way that benefits us, we are living in a "winning" way; when we don't make the most of our personalities, we are living in a "losing" way.

About 30 percent, or less than a third, of people today have one pure face shape, according to my personal observations. I'd estimate that about 45 percent of faces combine two shapes.

Sometimes the shapes are side by side, with one type on the left and the other on the right. Some faces are double-decker, with one shape on the bottom and another on top. Still others are a mix of characteristics—the permutations are endless. The ancients were certainly familiar with such combinations, even if they were much less common.

Some 15 to 20 percent of the faces I read are combinations of three face shapes. Some of the more familiar combinations have been inducted into the system and named. For example, the Jade, King, and Fire mix is known as the Dragon face. But many combinations are novel, and for those the face reader must describe all three. Such evaluations are very challenging because it can be hard to know which face is dominant. One day (or to one face reader), the person may present as a Tree; on another (or to a different reader), as a Bucket face; and so on. Not surprisingly, those who incorporate three face types very often feel misunderstood. The contradictory responses of others tend to make them question who, in fact, they are.

The benefit of having three face shapes is flexibility. Because these people have faces suited for so many different scenarios, they are highly adaptable. The flipside of that adaptability is confusion, because when you tread firmly everywhere, it's tough to find your true path. To live in a winning way, the person with three face shapes must cultivate the winning qualities of at least the dominant face, if not all three.

Only 5 to 10 percent of people I see combine four or more face shapes. There's a name for this phenomenon: the Master of Masks. Such people are torn—they are so highly receptive that they may not recognize (if they can even imagine having) their authentic selves. Typically, they're plagued by mood swings and other mental complications. Imagine the stress of identifying with everyone and yet no one—say, of feeling the compulsion to take charge while being driven to tolerate and empathize. It's as if they have a superpower that's always thrumming, so they can never find peace.

Used in a losing way, this superpower can make them master manipulators, since they can get inside so many people's heads. Living in a winning way, they can become genius actors, capable of brilliantly creating a range of characters, or mentors, uniquely able to understand, uplift, and inspire. Those who seek readings are usually enlightened enough to know who they are, but they invariably ask, "What should I be?" It takes a lot of rigor and insight to find the answer.

What follows are the basic face shapes—the first four being the most common today—and the qualities associated with them.

Jade Face

Jade faces are very common, especially in Asia. In the West, most of the pure Jade faces I see are women, with just a handful of men showing up in my sessions each year. Jade faces seem to appear more often than others in combinations, so there are many Jade Trees and Jade Kings around.

People with Jade faces are usually eye-catching, with full lips, delicate noses, and a seductive gaze. Their faces are somewhat heart-shaped, with a wider forehead and a rounded chin. They have a positive outlook and are good at friendship. Men with Jade faces make even better partners or mates than they do friends.

When they're young, Jade faces are often underestimated or even treated like children, so they don't tend to come into their own until their later years. Their life mission is to resist anyone or any situation that makes them feel "small"—undervalued or diminished.

The characteristics of the Jade face include:

- Appreciation of beauty, style, and quality
- Love of nature and peace
- Vivid imagination
- Enthusiasm, passion, romance
- Open-mindedness and eagerness to learn

When living in a *winning* way, Jade faces are:

- Soulful and spirited, openly expressing their enthusiasm
- Fully rounded: imaginative, immersed in beauty and loving friendships

When living in a *losing* way, Jade faces are:

- Indecisive and timid
- Too willing to compromise, for fear of conflict
- Constantly complaining and criticizing, while oversensitive to others' slights
- Rejecting and unforgiving

King Face

King faces are also very common. Consulting for corporations and law enforcement, I see an especially high proportion, since they tend to gravitate to positions of power. In recent years, I've seen an increase in the number of female King faces. Usually, female King faces are in the top echelons of companies, while male Kings are more scattered throughout the hierarchy, where they may be comfortable serving a higher King or else jockeying for position.

The King face is typically angular, with a strong jawline and a prominent chin, cheekbones, and forehead. Often there is a single "power wrinkle" in one cheek. The eyes are usually small and deep-set, and the lower lip tends to be fuller than the upper.

King faces make better leaders than followers and are wired to act rather than react. They have strong caretaking instincts and therefore are very protective of underlings, children, and other "little people," as well as animals.

The characteristics of the King face include:

- Discernment and connoisseurship, a love of the finer things
- Desire for variety in sexual partners and experiences
- A thirst for knowledge

- The tendency to go to extremes
- Belligerence when young and patriarchal traits with age

When living in a *winning* way, King faces:

- Defend the weak and the vulnerable
- Are strong, decisive leaders, with talent for motivating others
- Are passionate and engaging, spreading joy
- Make excellent parents
- Invest effort in building strong and lasting relationships

When living in a *losing* way, King faces:

- Can be intolerant, dogmatic, and stubborn
- Have a tendency to abuse drugs and alcohol
- May cheat on their spouses or partners
- Can be aggressive—in the worst-case scenario, to the point of violence

Fire Face

The Fire face is somewhat triangular, with a wide forehead like the Jade face, but with a pointed chin. People with Fire faces are usually very attractive and passionate. They love others but also very much want to be loved.

Fire faces are often plagued with self-doubt. They have high expectations of themselves. They can be quite confident when young, but later in life may find it hard to trust others.

The characteristics of the Fire face include:

- Enthusiasm for learning, ability to grasp a situation
- Curiosity and love of travel
- Impulsiveness and quickness
- Attention seeking, which can be hard to ignore
- Being demanding of themselves and others

When living in a *winning* way, Fire faces are:

- Self-assured, vibrant, and passionate
- Quick to master and apply knowledge
- Instinctual and able to rely on their instincts
- Strongly supportive of others, especially emotionally

When living in a *losing* way, Fire faces:

- Doubt themselves and mistrust others
- Are highly distractible, scattered, and unable to focus
- Can be impatient, controlling, and manipulative
- Can be narcissistic or self-involved

Tree Face

Tree faces are long and wide, usually with a U shape line running from the corners of the mouth to beneath the chin. Tree faces tend to be reliable and rooted, set in their ways. Though they like to be surrounded by people, they may find it hard to connect emotionally with others. They protect and comfort others but cherish their independence.

The characteristics of the Tree face include:

- Caring for and protecting others
- Loyalty and reliability
- Rootedness, resistance to change
- The need for clarity and plans, rather than improvisation
- Being a lone wolf, despite the need for company
- Pensiveness, even brooding, and reluctance to share feelings

When living in a *winning* way, Tree faces:

- Make others feel secure, safe, and sheltered
- Smooth the way for others with their foresight and planning
- Are thoughtful, trustworthy, and reliable

When living in a *losing* way, Tree faces:

- Struggle in life, resist tackling their own problems, and often fail to achieve their own goals
- Make too many sacrifices for others, to the point of burnout
- Try to boost their energy with sweets, tobacco, and alcohol

Moon Face

The Moon face looks just as it sounds: big and round, often shiny, set in a circular head. The mouth in a Moon face is usually large, with lips of any size, as if designed for communication and socializing. That's what Moon faces like best: partying and entertaining.

Moon faces are colorful, humorous lovers of fun, but they can also be loyal friends. They need personal space and a solid foundation—a settled career, a mate, and a nurturing home, which they tend to establish early in life. The challenges for a Moon face are to resist pleasure seeking, develop responsibility, and take the lead rather than follow the whims of others. Also, they need to retreat from the limelight enough to stay grounded and find happiness not in the acclaim of others but within themselves.

The characteristics of the Moon face include:

- Pleasure seeking, curiosity, and humor
- Conviviality, the ability to charm and entertain
- Loyalty in friendship, the need for a solid home base
- A tendency to live on applause, rather than to develop their own sense of worth

When living in a *winning* way, Moon faces:

- Are the life of the party, gracious hosts, welcome guests
- Are genuine lovers of people, great communicators, and faithful friends
- Are generous in uplifting and making social connections for others
- Have an eye for quality and fully enjoy life

When living in a *losing* way, Moon faces:

- Lack discipline and tend to overdo pleasure seeking
- May be deeply wounded by public criticism, puncturing their social façade
- May deploy their humor as vicious sarcasm
- May suffer from self-doubt and allow others to dominate them
- May lose themselves in the limelight and the clutter of shallow friendships, failing to look within to find happiness

Bucket Face

The Bucket face has a flowerpot shape, with a squared, straight-across chin and the sides of the face angling up to a wider forehead. Other distinguishing characteristics include dreamy, half-lidded eyes and a full mouth, bracketed by nasolabial folds or wrinkles stretching from the sides of the nose all the way down to the chin.

The designation Bucket face may sound pedestrian, but people of this type are anything but—they're highly original and talented, with the capacity to combine creativity and pragmatism. They're visionaries who want to build to last and to leave a legacy. They have the power to motivate and inspire others. One thing they don't do well is fire up their own creative intelligence. They need a muse of some kind, like a lover or a teacher or an environment that somehow sparks them. They are lost without that ignition.

The characteristics of the Bucket face include:

- Creativity and originality
- Having dreamy but practicable visionary ideas
- The need for a trigger or a muse to fire them up

When living in a ***winning*** way, Bucket faces:

- Are flooded with imaginative visions and creative intelligence
- Have the power to fire others' enthusiasm for their ideas
- Have the talent and drive to realize their dreams

When living in a ***losing*** way, Bucket faces:

- Can't mobilize their own energies
- Can feed off or burn out the other people they use to ignite or execute their visions
- Follow the lead of the others rather than generate their own creative thinking

Mountain Face

The Mountain face is pear-shaped, fuller at the jowls than at the forehead, which has a characteristic slope. Chinese tradition holds that Mountain faces "go the long path," meaning that they're usually late bloomers and may reach an advanced age. It also suggests that they have their own concept of time, so they rarely hurry and tend to put things off. With their elastic view of time, they never forget a favor or lose a grudge.

Being on the long path, focused on the future, they don't get stuck in setbacks, health or otherwise, but are quick to rebound. Chinese teachings warn them to prepare for the future by choosing to "speak from the happy mountain" instead of the "lonely mountain"—to cultivate meaningful experiences and relationships that can endure for the long haul.

The characteristics of the Mountain face include:

- Patience, being painstaking, but also procrastination
- Strong communication skills but a tendency to withhold thoughts and feelings
- Being an unapologetic loner, though capable of lifelong friendships
- Pleasure seeking

When living in a *winning* way, Mountain faces:

- Use their strong memory to benefit themselves and others
- Have the patience and endurance to wait out problems and let them resolve
- Are resilient, springing back from defeats
- Are generous with their time and resources and can be good mentors

When living in a *losing* way, Mountain faces:

- Hold grudges, are unforgiving and intolerant
- Procrastinate and leave important tasks undone
- Withhold feelings, can be asocial and withdrawn

Ground or Earth Face

The Ground face is shaped like a pyramid with the top cut off—as broad as it is tall, wider at the jawline than at the forehead. The jaws are strong and square or sometimes accentuated with a squared beard. Ground faces look bullish, which reflects their determined, forceful nature. With single-minded focus, they muscle aside people and obstacles in their way. As movers and shakers, they can be overconfident and blind to errors. They can also be so self-absorbed as to barely acknowledge others. Their life challenge is to cultivate humility and openhearted caring.

The characteristics of the Ground face include:

- Lively curiosity, great thirst for knowledge
- Great energy, drive, and confidence
- Laser focus toward a goal
- A lone wolf nature, estranged from and sometimes competitive with others

When living in a **winning** way, Ground faces:

- Are dynamic, engaged, and decisive and quick to make things happen

- Are eager to learn, curious, open to new ideas
- Exude confidence and command, empower those who are weaker
- Have a strong drive, as well as single-minded focus and determination and are highly likely to achieve

When living in a *losing* way, Ground faces:

- Can be ill-tempered and bullying to the point of cruelty
- Tend to steamroll others who are in their way
- Can be overconfident and stubborn, with tunnel vision, blind to their own weaknesses
- Have no respect for or interest in other people

Iron Face

The Iron face looks, at first glance, like a squared-off Moon face: it is relatively flat, with prominent cheeks, a small nose, and a thin-lipped mouth that is either exceptionally long or short. People with Iron faces are solid—calm, unshakeable, and even fearless, reliable, judicious in decision-making, firm in their opinions, tough and resilient, supportive and loyal. They risk becoming stolid—set in their ways, fatalistic, sluggish to the point of inertia. The life mission of an Iron face is to let go of responsibility, reach out for life's pleasures, and keep moving and growing.

The characteristics of the Iron face include:

- Composure, steadfastness, reliability
- Rationality, well-reasoned decision-making
- Toughness and resilience
- Loyalty and supportiveness
- A dry sense of humor

When living in a *winning* way, Iron faces:

- Are unflappable, even in a crisis
- Approach decisions by weighing all facts
- Are focused and persistent in pursuing goals
- Are steadfast, reliable, and responsible to a fault
- Are trustworthy and loyal, building lifelong friendships

When living in a *losing* way, Iron faces:

- Can be indecisive and grow sluggish to the point of inertia
- Can be too trusting, too loyal, and hyper-responsible, clinging to people, tasks, and ideas that no longer benefit them
- Can weaponize their razor-sharp wit
- Can grow fatalistic and resistant to change

Wall Face

Wall faces, seen more often in Asia, are relatively rare in the Western world. The Wall face is broader than it is long. In my mind, I see it as a hammerhead, both because of its shape and because of the implied fix-it abilities. Wall faces are highly pragmatic, usually good with their hands, and love to solve straightforward problems, like home repairs. More complex situations may discombobulate them. They can be very creative, but only if they have a goal.

Wall faces typically are uncommunicative and so emotionally reserved that they are hard to befriend. They prefer to avoid interacting with other people and thus resist social gatherings. They can be painfully blunt. On the other hand, they are good neighbors—always willing to help with practical matters—and are reliable and true to their word. The life challenges for Wall faces are to free their own creativity by doing work for its own sake, without a goal; to indulge impulses now and then; and to invest more of their considerable energy in others—in short, to get out of their own way.

The characteristics of the Wall face include:

- Practicality, rationality, and reliability
- Creativity in solving straightforward problems

- A neutral, unemotional affect
- Discomfort with human connections, especially in social gatherings
- Unfiltered frankness, coupled with acceptance of candid criticism

When living in a *winning* way, Wall faces:

- Are reliable and true to their world
- Have stamina, persistence, and resilience
- Are generous with their time and problem-solving ability
- Manage to come out of their shell to connect with and support others
- Accept constructive criticism and temper their own bluntness
- Grow by getting in touch with their own creativity

When living in a *losing* way, Wall faces:

- Are self-involved and asocial, closed off from the world
- Hurt others through social clumsiness and insensitivity
- Cannot cope with their own feelings or connect emotionally with others
- Are too goal-oriented to freely express their creativity
- Hold themselves back, living imprisoned by their own social and imaginative limitations

Some Combination Faces. Left to right: Jade King Face, Jade Moon Face, Fire Tree Face

II. Elements of the Face

The "Personality Regions" illustration (on the following page), drawn from the ideas of Aristotle and his disciples, shows how the ancient Greeks linked areas of the face to personality. It parallels the Palaces of Luck system in Chinese face reading that we discussed in chapter 4. A difference is that the Palaces of Luck system varies by region, masters, and other factors, including issues that clients want to explore, but the European system is fixed. It is also less predictive, focused more on describing the client at a given time than on forecasting the future.

It's important to note that the regions associated with realms of life like decision-making, work, and intimacy are merely focal points for examining those areas. It is essential to study the entire face and all its unique features and qualities to develop a meaningful sense of a given human being.

Whether or not the Asian and European systems have common roots is a matter of debate, but the fact that similar methods of personality assessment arose on different continents shows the universality of face reading.

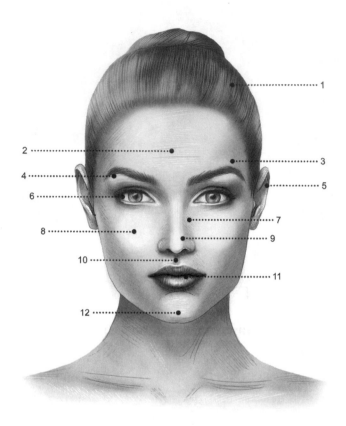

The Personality Regions of the Face. 1. Nature, Sensations, Perceptions. 2. Interests. 3. Personality, Ideals. 4. Attitude. 5. Decision-Making, Sense of Reality. 6. Soul, Intimacy. 7. Work. 8. Leadership, Support. 9. Materialism. 10. Attraction. 11. Communication, Interests. 12. Morality, Engagement, Principles.

The Eyes

The eyes are the first features that draw us to a person, that bond us together, that let us communicate silently. They're directly linked to the brain by the optic nerve, a bundle of more than a million nerve fibers. When light hits the eye, the iris expands or constricts the pupils to control how much to admit. The lens of the eye focuses the light on the retina, which absorbs it and converts it to electrochemical impulses. Via the optic nerve, these impulses zip into the brain, which translates them into images we

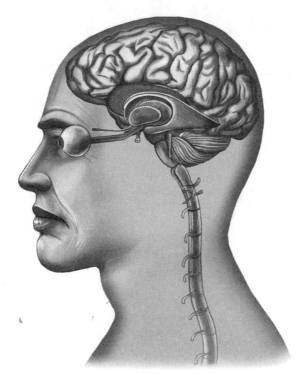

The Optic Nerve

can understand. This simplified explanation barely does justice to the complex, miraculous process that is vision—the primary way that we interact with the world. So, while it may be a cliché, it's no wonder that the eyes are called the window to the soul.

When face readers examine the eyes, one thing we don't consider is the color. Unless there's a strange imbalance—say, a change in hue or eyes of different colors, like David Bowie's, supposedly from a head blow—whether the eyes are brown, hazel, violet, blue, or green doesn't matter as much as the factors we'll discuss here and in "The Face of Health," on page 271.

Face readers examine the visible parts of the eye—namely, the sclera, iris, and pupil. All three offer important clues about a person's personality and well-being.

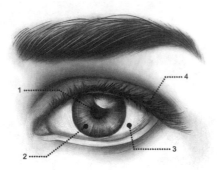

Parts of the Eye. 1. Pupil. 2. Iris. 3. Sclera. 4. Lashes.

THE SCLERA

The sclera is the white part of the eye. Its appearance—its color, its clarity, and how much of it is visible—is significant.

- *Sclera visible below the iris* can be a sign of physical or mental exhaustion. It can also indicate that the person is a dreamer whose mind is always somewhere else or who is overstimulated by his or her imagination.
- *Sclera visible above the iris* often suggests the person is consumed by negative emotions like fear, anger, or aggression. These feelings can flare in the moment, which is not unusual, but visible sclera above the iris as a chronic condition that can be the mark of a violent person.
- *Sclera visible below and above the iris,* which is less common, is a sign of hypersensitivity and hyperreactivity. It may occur occasionally under challenging conditions, such as when a person suffers extreme stress. But if this presentation is chronic, it is associated with high anxiety, mood swings, anger, and aggression. Control of feelings and decision-making will prove challenging. A person in this state is emotionally exhausted and may try to recharge through addictive behaviors or may simply withdraw from the world.

THE IRIS

The iris is the colored ring surrounding the pupil of the eye. Some believe that it holds important clues to health, but its study, iridology or iridiagnosis, remains somewhat controversial. The iris helps control the light-admitting functions of the pupil.

THE PUPIL

The pupil is the black center section of the eye, which contracts and expands to let in light. Highly expressive, it holds a wealth of information about a person's personality and state of health. To determine pupil size, we compare them to an average of those observed in the same environment and under the same light. Strong emotions and compelling thoughts can expand our pupils.

- *Large pupils,* sometimes called the mark of "lover's eyes," usually signify a warm, sympathetic nature and openness to others, keen intuition and the tendency to rely on gut feelings, strong emotions, spontaneity, creativity, dreaminess, excitability and fearfulness, reduced stamina, and an inclination toward melancholy and depression.
- *Small pupils* usually indicate a rational and analytic nature, an appreciation for creativity and feelings if grounded in facts, a tendency to worry and brood over problems, relative courage (but, when gripped with fear, unable to shake it), and, in general, difficulty relaxing and letting go.
- *Unbalanced pupils*—one large and one small—often signify physical pain. The enlarged pupil appears on the side of the body where the pain occurs. The location may be evident from the person's gait or posture, redness in areas of the face that correspond to organ systems, and so on.

258 Read the Face

DISTANCE BETWEEN THE EYES

Whether the eyes are close together or far apart may reveal how well a person can concentrate and focus.

- *Narrow distance between the eyes* implies the ability to focus, to zero in on a point or a topic; the tendency to concentrate attention in a few areas, studying every detail; pragmatic thinking; and, sometimes, narrow-mindedness.
- *Wide distance between the eyes* implies a romantic disposition; openness to the new and a relaxed view of life; the tendency to get overwhelmed and unable to focus, lost in details; an aspiration to leadership, often unfulfilled through self-denial.

DEPTH OF THE EYES

Every skull has the same kind of holes, so eyes that seem more protruding or deep-set than average may reflect personality tendencies.

- *Protruding eyes* are a well-known sign of thyroid disorder, but they may also indicate a full engagement in life, with a network of involvements, and an aversion to being distracted or interrupted.
- *Deep-set eyes* may indicate a skeptical and critical nature, superficial involvement in the world, maintenance of a façade to shield true emotions, vulnerability to ridicule, and the tendency to poke at and expose the vulnerabilities of others.

ORIENTATION OF THE EYES

Since eye sockets are all of roughly the same shape, the way the eyes are oriented is clearly influenced by the brain and, thus, is meaningful to face readers. By orientation, I mean the way the outer corners point—neutral, upward, or downward. It's even possible for the eyes to be mismatched, with just one corner pointing upward or downward. Conceivably, the outer corners of mismatched eyes could point in different directions—one up, one down—but I have never seen that.

- *Outer corners point upward.* These are the eyes we see in comic book heroes, tricksters, and villains. Art imitates—in this case, exaggerates—life. Often called "cat eyes," this shape signifies the drive to act, a fiery temperament, extroversion, and the dislike of being alone. (You won't see a cat-eyed person on a meditation retreat.) In comic books—and, to some extent, in life—whether the cat-eyed person is a charismatic force for good, a fun friend, or an evildoer depends on other elements in the face, especially the mouth. A smiling mouth could be a friendly sign, an impression refined by looking at its shape and other features, while a frown could spell trouble.

- *Outer corners point downward.* In comic books, eyes with outer corners slanting downward could mark the hapless victim, the defeated sadsack, the dopey guy, the follower—no leader would ever be depicted this way—or the melancholic, even the depressive. But when paired with a smiling mouth, eye corners pointing downward can convey a warm, sympathetic, or even sentimental image. When I have such a client, I know that the person will listen carefully to my observations and take them to heart, unlike the cat-eye client, who's likely to need convincing.

- *Mismatched outer corners.* Sometimes we see the outer corner of just one eye slanting upward or downward. If it's on the right, the eye governed by the left or conscious, analytic side of the brain, an upturn might mean being logically or intellectually aggressive, while a downturn might imply being defensive. If it's on the left, the eye ruled by the right or unconscious, feeling side of the brain, an upturn might imply restless creativity, while a downturn could indicate depression. In both cases, the other, neutral eye would remain more flexible and respond normally to stimuli.

- **Outer corners neutral.** The most common orientation, neutral eyes, have straight outer corners, roughly aligned with the inner corners. Such eyes indicate flexibility—that the person isn't predisposed to being active or passive, extroverted or shy, intense or depressive.

EYELIDS

Most unusual characteristics of the upper and lower eyelids are related to physical conditions, as discussed in "The Face of Health," on page 271. But one trait we commonly see that's connected to personality is half-lidded eyes. These upper eyelids are not puffy or slack from connective-tissue weakness but are simply at half-staff—tightly fitting but, when open, half covering the eyeball. They look like the eyes of Garfield, the lazy cartoon cat, who also has the large pupils of a pleasure seeker. Such half-lidded eyes are the mark of the daydreamer, the imaginative thinker lost in his or her own mind.

EYELASHES

We all have long eyelashes when we're very young, which we tend to lose over the years. So, for a face reader, long eyelashes in an adult suggest that person retains some childlike qualities, like vitality and heightened sensitivity. That sensitivity makes the person easy to startle or frighten. In every culture, the longer the eyelashes, the more attractive the person is considered to be.

The Mouth

According to an Asian proverb, "The mouth is the portal to happiness." It's interesting to think about why: we use it for sustenance and for what I call the three *c*'s: creativity, communication, and kissing (which begins with the same sound, though spelled with a *k*). People wear lipstick and plump up their lips with fillers to advertise that they're good at the three *c*'s. But in evaluating the mouth, face readers make a distinction between the opening itself and the lips. The factors we consider are the size of the mouth; the fullness, proportion, and shape of the lips; and the orientation of the mouth's corners.

SIZE OF THE MOUTH

The size of the mouth corresponds to the degree of attention a person needs and can also reveal how he or she interacts with others. The mouth is measured from corner to corner of the opening, which may or may not be the same length as the lips.

- A *large mouth* shows that a person is extroverted and enjoys commanding the spotlight. Those with large mouths are comfortable talking to anyone and radiate an inviting openness, friendliness, and energy. However, they may be too quick to tell people what they want to hear.
- A *small mouth* shows that a person dislikes being the focus of attention. Rather than chatter, people with small mouths choose their words carefully and fare better in serious discussions than at small talk. They tend not to be good flatterers or liars and tend to remain silent rather than stretch the truth.
- A *medium mouth* shows that a person is flexible and able to communicate easily and effectively, both one-on-one and at center stage. While valuing truth telling, the

medium-mouth person has a special talent for fibbing when necessary.

FULLNESS OF THE LIPS

Whether a person's lips are considered full or thin depends on how they relate to the rest of the face, not how they compare to the lips of others. The fullness of the lips indicates how open or closed someone is and how likely they are to be personally revealing. They also reflect how much someone allows himself or herself to act on or realize wishes and desires.

- *Full-lipped people* are inclined to expose their private inner worlds, confiding feelings, desires, and personal experiences and inviting the same openness from others. They have strong persuasive powers and also an unconscious tendency to put others on the spot.
- *Thin-lipped people* tend to be closemouthed, not revealing much of themselves and even consciously keeping secrets. When speaking, they don't ramble but get to the point quickly. If they get verbose or talk fast, chances are that they're nervous or trying to hide something. They tend to be ungenerous and to judge others according to the belief that we each forge our own destiny.

PROPORTIONS OF THE LIPS

The proportions of the lips, or the fullness of one relative to the other, often reveal whether people prefer to discuss facts or feelings.

- A *full upper lip* suggests that a person would talk about ideas and emotions rather than the material world. People with full upper lips can also be extraordinarily empathetic.

However, they tend to be very talkative, which can annoy those around them.

- A *full lower lip* indicates that a person prefers conversation that's focused on facts and events, rather than feelings.

SPECIAL SHAPES OF THE LIPS

Lips with special shapes, in face-reading lingo, are those with uncommon dimensions or qualities. Whether they're long or short and thin or full and whether they run the whole length of the mouth are among the factors determining what they reveal about a person. Very pliable and rubbery, lopsided, or deeply lined lips also convey specific information.

- *Very long, full lips,* known as the "lips of love," signify communication, creativity, and feelings. People with such lips love to make grand gestures, confide their thoughts, and lavish attention on others. They tend to prefer giving over taking.
- *Very long, thin lips,* in Germany, are known as the "millionaire's mouth," probably because they indicate preoccupation with the material world. People with such lips are usually great communicators but avoid emotional discussions and disclosures.
- *Short, very full lips* imply that a person tends to tell the truth. People with such lips value their privacy and usually divulge important matters only to close friends.
- *Short, thin lips* suggest that a person is more withdrawn and likely to conceal feelings, even from those closest to them. Such people may tend to harbor resentment. When they do speak, they can astutely identify the heart of a problem, and their well-chosen words carry weight for those around them.

- *Long mouth, short lips*—in this configuration, the lips appear to bunch at the center of a wide opening. People with such lips are usually secretive and hide information not just from others but sometimes even from themselves. They can be good advisers—dispassionate and discreet—or entertaining, in a low-key way.

- *Rubbery lips*, very animated in motion, indicate gregariousness, a love of self-expression. People with rubbery lips can be very impulsive and often frustrated.

- *Lopsided lips* signify that a person is plagued with insecurities and has trouble trusting others. Such people tend to be intensely passionate but also very jealous.

- *Closed lips* have a few deep lines running though them, from the level of the philtrum to above the chin. These lines are different from the row of short, fine wrinkles often seen above the upper lip in older women, signifying the loss of estrogen. Instead, they look almost as if the mouth had been sewn shut with one to six large stitches. What these lines reveal is hardship in life, whether privation over the years or some kind of trauma, which has, in effect, sealed the mouth, preventing discussion of difficult experiences and emotions.

CORNERS OF THE MOUTH

The corners of the mouth are a critical element for face readers because they hold the key to a person's basic nature. In most people, the mouth corners turn upward or lie in a neutral position, pointing straight into the cheeks, when at rest. But the fact that a person's nature is "basic," or fundamental, doesn't mean that it's immutable. Over the years, it can change. Frequent laughter—even a fake grin every day—can reset a person's attitude, causing the corners of the mouth to turn upward.

- *. **Downturned corners of the mouth** signify a nature that's pessimistic or even gloomy. People with downturned corners tend to have a diminished sense of well-being and to anticipate worst-case scenarios. Whether because of some particular anguish or grief or simply because they see no reason to be cheerful, they always look on the dark side.

- **Upturned corners of the mouth** signify a fundamental nature that's cheerful, curious, optimistic, and confident about the future. People with upturned corners are energetic and active, fully engaged with life and inclined toward joy.

The Forehead

Who we are and how we think, as a German expression holds, "is written on the forehead." It's like a placard that presents the personality to the outside world, so it's worth offering some basic guidelines about what it shows. The eyes and mouth create the portrait of a person, but the forehead can help confirm an initial impression, provide insight into observed contradictions, or sketch in missing detail.

As a general rule, most facial lines above the eyes relate to personality and its development over the course of our lives. Forehead lines can reveal efforts we've made, consciously or unconsciously, to integrate our personality and our character. The shape of the forehead, as well as the number and nature of wrinkles on it, holds meaning for the face reader.

FOREHEAD SHAPE

The terms "high" and "low" in reference to the forehead are based on the amount of space between the eyebrows and the hairline; "narrow" or "broad" refers to the measurement from temple to temple.

- A **high** forehead may indicate high intelligence and shrewdness, since many associate it with greater brain volume.
- A **low** forehead may indicate lack of foresight and tendency to get in trouble, as well as, to some people's minds, a lack of charisma.
- A **broad** forehead may indicate foresight, the tendency to plan ahead, open-mindedness, and tolerance.
- A *narrow* forehead may indicate lack of tolerance and limited thinking, as well as likeliness to assume the opinions of others.

FOREHEAD WRINKLES: HORIZONTAL

Not everyone has the same number or type of forehead wrinkles. Normally, there are three main horizontal lines, each of which are associated with various areas of life. In general, the more wrinkles there are in the forehead, the more complex the personality. While forehead lines are most clearly visible in older adults, they may also be present in younger people when they frown. Some Chinese readers believe forehead lines are present in babies but fade and then re-form based on life experience.

The three main horizontal lines, plus another common type of wrinkle, are:

- The **bottom** line, closest to the eyebrows, which relates to the material world
- The **middle** line, which relates to the self or the ego
- The **uppermost** line, closest to the hairline, which relates to creativity, idealism, and spiritual life
- **Instinct** or **intuition** lines, which many people have, appear above each eyebrow and form if the person has a lot of *aha!* moments that prompt them to literally or figuratively raise their eyebrows, as if to say, "I get it!"

The depth and length of each line signifies the importance that the realm it governs has in the person's life. For example, a person with just one forehead line or a very prominent one close to the eyebrows is consumed by everyday life rather than by pursuing self-knowledge or abstract spiritual ideas. The other lines may deepen as the person develops the related interests.

- *Three horizontal lines of approximately equal length and depth* indicate that a person is centered, with a distinct personality and diverse interests, and welcomes challenges.

- *Unbroken or continuous horizontal lines* indicate that the person is balanced in a given realm and can solve problems quickly.

- *Broken or interrupted horizontal lines* indicate that the person has unresolved issues in a given realm. Such a person may have many interests but lack the focus to consistently pursue or complete things. He or she may be a continual seeker, always looking for the right life path and questioning or regretting past directions.

- *A few horizontal lines amid the main ones* reflect issues or interests that the person is pursuing. Lines that are mostly straight but extend a short distance indicate issues that the person is working on; when they stretch farther, they show that the work is completed. Sometimes these lines originate in the center of the forehead and stretch toward the temples. If lines start on the left, they indicate that the issue emanates from the subconscious, creative realm, and those starting from the right emerge from the logical, material realm.

- *Many scattered, randomly angled lines* signify that the person is what Chinese face readers call a "flying bird." Such people are often vibrant and fascinating because they have so many interests, but they never "alight on one tree" long enough to pursue them. Flying birds are usually not good prospects for long-term commitments.

FOREHEAD WRINKLES: VERTICAL

Vertical lines on the forehead, or *vertical glabellar wrinkles*, start at the bridge of the nose and run between the eyebrows, toward the hairline. The skull is slightly depressed between the eyebrow ridges in this area, which is called the glabella. In the Chinese Mien Shiang school of face reading, as well as in the ancient system of physiognomy, these lines are viewed as significant markers of character or even destiny.

Interestingly, in old statues and portraits, we rarely see vertical glabellar wrinkles. Not only do they seem to be a fairly modern development, they are more common in the Western world than in the East and in the Northern Hemisphere than in the Southern. That suggests that in the more industrialized areas of the earth, people think differently—perhaps more analytically and strategically.

The categories of these lines include:

- *Parallel vertical glabellar wrinkles,* which are straight, are also called "scowl" or "thinking" lines, because they develop over years of intense concentration, critical analysis, or brooding. They're often present in those who tend to think hard before making a decision.
- *Reversed glabellar wrinkles* are arcs that curve outward, so that their most rounded segments are closest together. They can indicate a fearful nature and difficulty in maintaining convictions.
- *Inverted V-shaped glabellar wrinkles* are straight and grow toward each other, in the shape of a volcanic cone. They

signify a strong sense of self-worth and possibly a "me-first" attitude.

- An ***individual vertical forehead furrow*** between the brows is called the "hanging needle." It's often seen in high achievers because it signifies a strong will, strong drive, and hard work. However, it may also indicate the degree of egotism, disregard for others, and, sometimes, a risk aversion that may sabotage success.

- ***Uneven vertical glabellar wrinkles*** are not an official category, but it's worth noting that lines of appreciably different length may hint at what a person is thinking: a long line on the left suggests more of a preoccupation with feelings, and on the right with logic and analysis.

The Hands

Face readers refer to the hands as the "second face," not because we analyze the lines, as palm readers do, but because their shape and the way they move can reflect our personalities in action. Whatever we want to accomplish, the hands execute. They have twenty-seven bones and thirty-three muscles, making them exquisitely expressive and sensitive. We bend and stretch our fingers, by some estimates, 25 million times in the average lifespan.

Study of the hand, or chirology, originated in India several thousand years ago and spread to China, Tibet, Persia, and Egypt. When it reached Europe, Aristotle became an advocate. From then on until the nineteenth century—except for a time when the Catholic Church suppressed it as "pagan"—chirology was deemed a serious science. A number of medical issues—gout, for example—do show up in the hands.

We intuitively recognize the importance of hands when we meet people. Surveys have shown that, after we scan the face, our eyes go to the hands. This is especially true of women. Maybe checking the hands is an adaptive behavior, as shaking hands is said to be—ensuring that the other person poses no threat. For face readers, the hands are helpful only as backup, to confirm or further inform what we see in the facial features. For us, what the face reveals is more meaningful than the shape of the hands.

The four basic hand types are labeled Earth, Air, Fire, and Water. This designation comes from the ancient Greek system developed by Empedocles and bears no relation to the time-honored Chinese theories of the elements.

- The **Earth hand** has wide, square palms, with a few well-defined lines and thick fingers the same length or shorter than the palm. The skin may be thick or ruddy. The person with Earth hands is usually a hard worker—highly pragmatic, organized, and determined; reliable and solid. Though creative and good with their hands, some are a bit earthbound and may benefit by stimulating their imagination.
- The **Air hand** also has a square palm, often with a web of deep lines, and long, thin fingers. People with Air hands are typically dynamic, vibrant, and easily bored. They tend to be curious, even intellectual—driven more by knowledge and logic than by emotion. Lively communicators, they often punctuate what they say with waving hands.
- The **Fire hand** has a long, rectangular palm, often etched with a tangle of lines, and short fingers. People with Fire hands are warmhearted, passionate extroverts—often popular because they're tolerant of others and true to their word. Restless and determined, they constantly seek creative challenges and risk burnout if not careful to manage stress.
- The **Water hand** has a long, sometimes oval-shaped palm,

with fine, orderly lines, and long, rounded or curved fingers. Those with Water hands tend to be sensitive, curious, and receptive—quick to grasp information. Lovers of art, music, and nature, they are often dreamers and may be prone to mood swings.

III. The Face of Health

Thousands of years ago, before microscopes and X-ray machines, face reading was a primary method of medical diagnosis. Over the millennia, many different traditions have developed, from European facial diagnosis to Indian Ayurveda and, of course, the

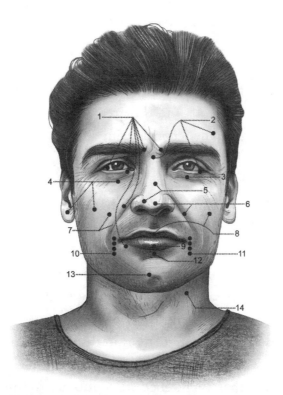

The Health Regions of the Face. 1. Liver. 2. Thyroid. 3. Bladder. 4. Kidneys. 5. Lungs. 6. Stomach. 7. Heart. 8. Small Intestine. 9. Colon. 10. Spleen. 11. Spleen. 12. Bile. 13. Abdomen. 14. Thyroid.

Chinese system Mien Shiang. Today, integrative medicine, which combines allopathic (conventional Western) and alternative disciplines, incorporates a range of traditional methods in diagnosis and treatment, including face reading.

Obviously, it takes years of study to master the art and science of diagnosis, but what follows are some health concerns that face reading can reveal. It's important to note that just one unusual observation may not be solid evidence of a disorder. Any irregularity must be interpreted in the context of the person's other features.

Because the eyes and the mouth are the most telling parts of the face, we'll concentrate on the clues they reveal.

Note: the information in this section is not a substitute for the advice of a qualified health professional.

The Eyes

A face reader examines not just the sclera, iris, and pupil but also the upper and lower eyelids and the area around the eyes, as well as the person's gaze, when considering health. The first questions are whether the eyes are clear, bright, and seemingly alert; whether the sclera is white; and whether the pupils are dilated. An observed symptom is meaningful if it has persisted and is not just the result of an allergy attack or a few late nights.

- *Watery eyes* indicate weak nerves and most often appear in people who are sad, worried, or emotionally out of balance following a trauma. They may be accompanied by frequent mood swings or other changes in disposition.
- *Cloudiness* that develops from watery eyes may signify low vitality and thus heightened susceptibility to inflammation and infections.

THE SCLERA

In a healthy person, the sclera is usually white. Discolorations of the sclera indicate problems of varying severity, and if they don't disappear quickly, warrant a medical examination.

- **Reddish eyes** occur because of blood vessel expansion in the conjunctiva, which is the mucus membrane lining the eyelids and protecting the eyeball. This expansion may be due to an irritant like smoke or eyedrops, a cold, allergies, or an infection of the membrane, called conjunctivitis. Redness in only one eye is likely caused by some kind of irritant. Bloodshot eyes may be a symptom of alcohol abuse. If redness doesn't subside quickly or is accompanied by itching, burning, watering, or sensitivity to light, it may signify a more serious condition.

- **Red-veined eyes, burst veins,** or **red spots,** not accompanied by itching or burning, can be caused by foreign objects, vigorous rubbing, allergies, or even intense sneezing or coughing. Persistent small red vessels may be a sign of venous stasis, meaning that, for some reason, blood isn't freely moving out of the eye. Constantly recurring burst blood vessels can indicate high blood pressure.

- **Yellow eyes** (a condition called **jaundice)** are always cause for alarm. They indicate the buildup of a bilirubin, a pigment created by red-cell breakdown, in the blood, usually because of a malfunction of the liver or gallbladder. The reasons for such malfunctions include hepatitis, cirrhosis, or cancer of the liver or pancreas. Yellow eyes call for immediate medical attention.

- **Brown spots** in the sclera also require swift medical attention. They may be the result of some past injury to the eye but often signify serious conditions, including acute gallbladder inflammation or liver diseases, such as hepatitis.

IRIS AND PUPILS

As discussed earlier in "Elements of the Face," eye color doesn't usually matter to face readers, but we do take notice when the irises are mismatched. The pupils hold much more significance, because they reflect both personality traits and health trends. The body's sympathetic nervous system expands the pupils, and in response to light the parasympathetic nervous system contracts them. Many drugs expand the pupils to the extent that even a flashlight waved before the eyes won't constrict them. Emotion, physical pain, and excessive consumption of alcohol also affect pupil size.

- *Eyes of different colors* may be the result of a harmless genetic disorder causing an uneven distribution of pigments. Though the eyes can be totally different—say, one blue and one brown—more often, one of the eyes has a blotch of a different color (sectoral heterochromia). Usually, the eyesight is not affected. Face readers consider those with mismatched eyes to be very sensitive, potentially subject to unstable moods and nervous disorders. However, in some cases, the difference results from illness, injury, or medications. An inflammation of the eye, for example, may cause the iris of that eye to grow paler.

- *Large pupils,* associated with emotionality, suggest that a person may suffer energy-sapping mood swings. People with large pupils may have slower lymphatic-system action, with symptoms like constipation and swollen glands, as well as circulatory problems and heart disease. They may also be prone to connective-tissue weakness, which affects skin and bones, and so may benefit from paying attention to the acid–alkaline balance in their diet (emphasizing plant over animal products).

- **Small pupils**, associated with brooding and worry, suggest susceptibility to muscle and joint problems, as well as vascular constriction and stress-related issues such as strokes.

COLORATION AND CROW'S-FEET
AROUND THE EYES

Many different conditions cause colorations and circles under the eyes, from insomnia to mineral deficiencies to skin conditions. The reason they appear is poor circulation in the thin skin around the eyes or, in some cases, too little oxygen in the blood. In children, shadows under the eyes can be a symptom of dehydration. The shade and appearance of colorations around the eyes offer clues as to their cause.

- **Thin, almost transparent skin around the eyes** may come with lack of sleep but may also indicate hormone changes, allergies, or eczema.
- **Reddish-brown coloration under or around the eyes** is often accompanied by the puffy or sagging skin that reflects buildup of metabolic waste products. It may become visible with age because thinning skin makes the color of the underlying blood vessels more obvious. People with reddish-brown circles tend to be rundown but restless and stressed and, as a result, feel emotionally out of balance.
- **Bluish or grayish coloration under or around the eyes,** along with puffiness, may be a sign of great fatigue, allergies like hayfever, or, like reddish-brown coloration, blood vessels visible through thinning skin. But another possible cause is persistent iron deficiency and, with it, a much weakened immune system. We often see bluish or grayish coloration

around the eyes in menstruating women or in people who are currently or have recently been ill.

- *Crow's-feet* or **laugh lines** are straight, fine wrinkles stretching from the outer corners of the eyes toward the temples. Because we feel the corners of our own eyes crinkle when we laugh, we associate the crow's-feet we see on other faces with amusement. So laugh lines appeal to us subconsciously. Some people are afraid to laugh for fear of deepening them, which is a misguided worry. Although they do come from years of scrunching up our faces, it's a combination of genetics and the mineral deficiencies that accrue with age, along with weakening connective tissue, that makes them grow. If they're very long and deep, they may signify great depletion of energy, as well as bigger connective-tissue issues like osteoporosis in women and hernias in men.

DEPTH OF THE EYES

Just as unusually bulging eyes or deep-set eyes reflect distinct personality traits, they may also offer important clues about health. Both cases need medical attention, because conditions that cause them can be serious.

- *Protruding eyes,* in extreme cases, may bulge out so far that the eyelids can no longer close completely. But even less dramatic presentations likely indicate that the immune system is attacking certain body structures, including fat stores behind the eyes and the ocular muscles, inflaming and enlarging them. Potential causes of protruding eyes are overactive thyroid disorders, such as Graves' disease, leukemia, and eye tumors.

- *Deep-set eyes* occur when the fat stores behind the eyes are depleted, possibly because of a serious condition, which can only be determined by a medical workup. Face readers associate them with very low energy reserves and caution those with deep-set eyes to avoid overexertion. Note that the combination of deep-set eyes and sinking temples can represent a life-threatening situation.

THE EYELIDS

With their thin, sensitive skin, the upper and lower eyelids are a barometer of health, both of the eyes and of other organ systems. Swollen upper eyelids and bags under the eyes can indicate anything from lack of sleep, crying, and overconsumption of alcohol or salt to disorders of the heart, gallbladder, and kidneys. Yellowish-white blobs under the eyes and close to the nose on the eyelids can be signs of liver or thyroid problems. Twitching eyelids can point to neurological disease. A skilled face reader may be able to interpret irregularities in the eyelids in conjunction with other signs on the face and body and help narrow down the possibilities. Medical tests may be needed to make a more precise determination of the causes. Here are some of the disorders the eyelids may reveal:

- *Swollen lower lids* or *bags under the eyes* are associated with such conditions as a heavy bout of tears, menstruation, a high salt intake, or medications that promote fluid retention. When these conditions change, the swelling may subside. More persistent swelling may result from sinus ailments; low thyroid function, especially if accompanied by fatigue; pregnancy; and problems with the uterus or prostate gland. Bladder and kidney disorders, such as renal insufficiency, are also possible causes, because the body is not eliminating water. If the lower eyelids have a purple-bluish color, a weak heart may be taxing the kidneys.

- *Swollen upper* or *so-called hooded eyelids* may not be as conspicuous as under-eye bags. Generally speaking, the periorbital area, or the region around the eyes, is one of the first places to show signs of aging, through sagging related to connective-tissue weaknesses. It is also associated with the body's fluid metabolism and waste management. Puffiness under the eyebrows is usually a sign of retained acidity. But swelling and slackness of the upper lids themselves may be related to the heart. They may signify venous return congestion, meaning that eye tissues are soaking up fluid not being pumped out because of heart diseases, such as valve defects or tamponade (accumulation of fluid around the heart, muffling its action), lung embolisms, and other serious conditions. If the heart is involved, there will be other physical symptoms, such as fluid retention in the hands, feet, ankles, and the back of the neck, especially in the evening.

- *Whitish-yellow fat deposits,* called *xanthelasmas,* are small clumps of nondegraded fats (cholesterol and lipids) that accumulate beneath the eyes and on upper lids close to the nose. They don't go away on their own and may indicate liver and gallbladder problems. They often occur in alcoholics and people with low thyroid function or fatty liver disease.

- *Twitches* or *irregular eyelid movements* are usually tics, or harmless muscle contractions typically affecting the lid (most often but not always the lower) of one eye. They may be caused by fatigue, stress, excessive caffeine, or too much time spent staring at a computer or television screen. Sometimes they result from lack of magnesium. But frequent and persistent twitches, especially if they encompass the face beyond the eyelids, should be checked by a doctor, since they may signify a neurological disorder. If accompanied by cramps in the hands and toes, stomachaches, sweating, rapid heart rate, or other disturbing symptoms, they may represent autonomic dystonia, caused by ailments ranging from diabetes and rheumatoid arthritis to cancer and Parkinson's disease.

Very infrequent eyelid movements, which may indicate low thyroid function, also warrant investigation.

THE GAZE

For Chinese Mien Shiang masters, the gaze is an important criterion of health, though its diagnostic value is less well understood in the West. The reason may be that interpreting the gaze requires rigorous training. Chinese masters assess the gaze from the point of their first eye contact with a person. A healthy gaze is clear and calm, with occasional, consistent blinking to keep the eye bathed in tear fluid. The atypical presentations, regarded as possible signs of illness, include the glossy, glassy, hollow, and dull gazes.

- The *glossy gaze* is watery, which is not the same as tearful. It signifies agitation—physical, such as feverishness, or emotional, such as intense excitement or anger. If the glossy gaze appears often, without an identifiable cause, it's an indication of weak nerves.
- The *glassy gaze* often follows the glossy gaze. It indicates that emotion has dissipated and thus the eyes look empty. It's a worrisome sign of physical weakness, such as a nutrient deficiency or the onset of illness.
- The *hollow gaze* is lifeless, without animation, as if there is no one behind the eyes. It's considered evidence of

problems in the intestines or some life-threatening process in the body.

- The *dull gaze* is characterized by eyes without luster, often hooded by the eyelids. It too indicates weakness, possibly serious, in the blood circulation or the heart.

THE EYEBROWS

Because they frame the eyes as part of the periorbital area that's so important in health evaluation, the eyebrows warrant discussion. Different types and placement of brows offer clues to the functions of the body's organ systems. The major classifications include bushy eyebrows; unibrows; and delicate, prematurely gray, and short eyebrows.

- *Bushy eyebrows,* which are wide, full, and shaggy, indicate an excess of male hormones. In women, they suggest weakness of the female organs and possibly premature menopause, especially when accompanied by a little mustache.
- *Unibrows* are brows connected across the bridge of the nose, which in some cases even look like a single band of hair. Aristotle believed them to be a sign of melancholy and grouchiness. Modern face readers say that they occur primarily in those who are strong willed and narrow-minded, qualities that correlate with headaches and high blood pressure. They may also signify vulnerability to blood circulation crises (apoplexy) and to epilepsy.
- *Delicate eyebrows,* narrow and fairly sparse, may be considered attractive in women but may indicate estrogen deficiency and painful menstruation. In men, they may suggest weakness of the male organs.
- *Prematurely gray eyebrows* have enough gray and white

hairs to give them a marked salt-and-pepper appearance. As we age, our eyebrows naturally turn gray as the body slows its production of melanin. But in young people, gray eyebrows are a warning sign of depression and even signal the risk of circulation disorders in the brain (cerebral sclerosis).

- **Short eyebrows** peter out partway above the eye rather than extend to the far corner or beyond. People with short eyebrows tend to have exaggerated expectations, which are often frustrated, making them irritable. Short eyebrows usually indicate endocrine disorders and suggest an inclination to gallbladder weakness. If the brows seem to stop abruptly, without tapering, or if the shorter hairs at the far corners fall out, the person may have an underactive thyroid gland.

The Mouth

The mouth, being the entry to the digestive tract, is a great source of information about the organs involved in processing our food and converting it to energy, such as the small and large intestines, stomach, spleen, pancreas, liver, and gallbladder. The factors that face readers consider include the color and shape of both lips (the lower offering insight into the large intestine, and the upper into the small intestine, which links it to the stomach); colorations of the skin, whether at the corners of the mouth or in thin lines above or below the lips; and wrinkles around the mouth. What follows are a few of the signs most meaningful for health.

THE LIPS

- **Swollen, bulging lips,** either one or both, often indicate an allergic reaction to foods, beverages, or cosmetics, especially if the swelling is accompanied by such symptoms as teary eyes, swollen mucus membranes, and red skin. Persistent swelling without a clear cause should be checked out since it may also be a symptom of neurological disease or, when the lower lip is swollen and crusted with red or white dots, an early stage of a particular skin cancer.

- *Very narrow, thin lips* show that a person has trouble letting go, both emotionally and physically, with regard to digestive and other functions. People with such lips have under-acidified stomachs, so they don't process food well and often feel uncomfortably full and gaseous. They're prone to intestinal inflammations that cause constipation or diarrhea. In old age, in many people, digestive activity slows down, which may be reflected in the thinning of their lips.

- *Blue lips* signify a lack of oxygen in the blood. The most common cause is exposure to cold temperatures, which constricts blood vessels in the lips. Intense emotional stress can have a similar effect, as can heavy smoking, carbon monoxide poisoning, and such respiratory ailments as asthma, bronchitis, and pneumonia. Blue lips are also a symptom of Raynaud's disease, which causes vasospasms: sudden blood vessel constrictions that can turn fingers, toes, nose, and ears numb and bluish pale for minutes or up to a few hours. Except when caused by exposure to cold (if lips quickly regain color after warming), blueness of the lips or any other part of the body is a condition called cyanosis and may indicate a medical emergency.

- A *whitish lower lip* doesn't have enough blood flowing through it to give it the usual reddish color. The whiteness might be just in places or along its entire length. The lack of color might indicate some deficiency in the blood or a low red blood cell count (anemia), possibly resulting from intestinal bleeding. Anything unusual about the lower lip—swelling, chapping, and the like—is worth noting.

- A **puffy-edged lower lip,** one that seems to have a narrow band of swelling below it, suggests problems with the detoxification organs of the body, especially the liver. The likely cause is abuse of alcohol and tobacco or difficulty processing some medication or foreign substance. Where the puffiness occurs along the edge of the lip points to the organ affected: swelling in the center implies the pancreas, distinct swelling at the right and left of center suggests the gallbladder, and swelling at the outer corners indicates the spleen. If the swelling persists, it's wise to consult a doctor.
- A **puffy-edged lower lip with pimples** in the chin area suggests the possibility of abdominal disorders or hormone imbalances. Sore areas under the nostrils would reinforce this impression.

DISCOLORATIONS AROUND THE MOUTH

- **Bluish coloring** around the mouth, as discussed in the "Lips" section above, is a sign of oxygen deprivation and requires medical attention.
- **Yellowish coloring** not on the lips but around the mouth indicates problems metabolizing fat and the inability of the intestine to tolerate high-fat foods.
- **Brownish coloring** around the mouth shows that the intestine is stressed by fermentation inside it or by ingested foreign substances or toxins.
- **Grayish coloring** around the mouth is usually seen in older people. It indicates that the muscles and other elements of the digestive tract no longer work as well and so it's harder to break down foods into accessible nutrients.

- *Red, sore corners of the mouth,* which may feature painful fissures or cracks, may be quite stubborn and slow to heal. They usually appear in those who are sickly and exhausted for reasons including thyroid disorders, iron-deficient anemia, and a severely depressed immune system struggling to combat bacteria, fungi, and viruses.

WRINKLES AROUND THE MOUTH

- *Fine vertical wrinkles above the upper lip* (and sometimes below the lower) appear only in women, never in men. We very often see them in a row of twenty or thirty in women of menopausal age because these lines are associated with depletion of the female hormone estrogen. If they show up in a young woman, there's cause for alarm because they indicate that her hormones are out of balance.

- *Individual vertical wrinkles above the upper lip,* as discussed on page 253 in "Elements of the Face," present as a few

A Face Showing Four Major Kinds of Wrinkles: Fine Vertical Wrinkles, Deep Vertical Wrinkles, Horizontal Wrinkle across the Philtrum, and Spleen Wrinkles

deep, coarse, vertical lines above the upper lip—often running through the lower as well, like stitches sewing the mouth shut—and are traditionally interpreted as evidence of a hard life. What they convey in terms of health is quite different: that not enough water gets from the stomach to the small intestine. Normally, the body keeps its intake, creation, and elimination of water in careful equilibrium, but these wrinkles occur when the water system is out of balance. Elimination of waste from the colon is affected, as are various other body functions.

- A *horizontal wrinkle above the upper lip*—that is, crossing the philtrum—is another line seen only in women. It can signify a past miscarriage or abortion, though not everyone who's had those experiences will bear such a mark. It's also a strong indication of back and joint problems, notably osteoporosis. It should be taken seriously if it appears along with other signs of osteoporosis, such as lines across the bridge of the nose and flaccid tissue, separate from the jowls, drooping between the chin and the neck.

- *Wrinkles stretching downward from the outer corners of the mouth* are called spleen lines, which may be accompanied by swelling around the eyes and in the neck and ankles. These wrinkles indicate that the spleen, which filters out and recycles old red blood cells as part of the immune system, is growing exhausted, often with age, so its detoxifying capacity is diminishing.

IV. Minerals

"The Face of Health" section, above, and various stories throughout the book discuss problems related to deficiencies of certain minerals we need to keep our bodies in balance. Since we can't produce these substances, we need to absorb them through our diet. There are two types of minerals we need:

- *Trace elements*, or *microminerals,* such as iron, fluoride, zinc, iodine, copper, chromium, manganese, and selenium
- *Volume elements,* or *electrolytes,* such as magnesium, potassium, calcium, sodium, bicarbonate, phosphate, and chloride

Causes of Imbalance

There are many possible causes of mineral imbalance or deficiency. Here are just a few examples:

- A limited diet (too much fast food, deprivation weight-loss regimens, insufficient intake of fruits and vegetables, etc.)
- Overconsumption of rich foods, tobacco, or alcohol (alcoholism is a major risk)
- Sedentary lifestyle
- Intense sweating or extreme physical activity
- Anorexia nervosa
- Hormonal disorders
- Illnesses
- Pregnancy and breastfeeding
- Menopause and other transitional stages associated with aging

Prevention and Treatment of Mineral Deficiency

Eating well and staying hydrated are the best ways to prevent mineral deficiencies:

- Drink plenty of water.
- Eat a balanced and varied diet, with an emphasis on fruits, vegetables, and whole grains.
- Steam rather than boil or fry foods in order to preserve their nutrients.
- Limit consumption of rich foods, sweets, sugary drinks, alcohol, tobacco, and processed meats, like sausages and cold cuts.

People who think they may have mineral deficiencies should check with a qualified healthcare provider, who may do appropriate testing before recommending a specific change of diet or food supplements. Note that the information in this section is not a substitute for the advice of a qualified health professional.

Symptoms of Imbalance

Mineral deficiencies and imbalances show up in too many ways to list exhaustively. Medical tests are necessary to determine the underlying cause of such symptoms as cramps, poor concentration and memory, reduced physical and mental capacity, fatigue and sleeplessness, nervousness, headaches, sweating, changes in the skin and hair, and so on. Face readers can detect certain signs of deficiency as a first step to determining the source of problems. "The Face of Health" section, on page 271, discusses the major signs of deficiency affecting our primary areas of concern, the eyes and mouth. Common signs affecting other parts of the face include:

- *Calcium-deficiency pallor.* Lack of calcium often shows up as an ashy whitening of the complexion and a waxy look, especially on the forehead and around the ears. The tongue often has a white coating. There may be horizontal lines across the bridge of the nose and, in advanced cases of deficiency, pouching around the jowls.
- *Magnesium-deficiency redness.* Lack of magnesium often causes facial reddening, starting as pinkish-red, coin-size blotches on the cheeks. These blotches can occur as a result of excitement, physical exertion, or a strong emotion such as stage fright. Other symptoms of a magnesium deficiency include cramps, muscle twitches, headaches, insomnia, and a craving for sweets.
- *Iron-deficiency redness.* Lack of iron tends to cause a different pattern of redness that spreads from the forehead or the ears, even reaching the cheeks if the deficiency is extreme.

Often, the person will have the sensation that the reddened skin is hot or "burning." Short-term redness will be most visible after physical exertion or being out in the cold. Long term, the redness suggests an imminent or present cold, flu, or fever. Other symptoms of iron deficiency include trouble sleeping, listlessness, fatigue, morning grumpiness, and diarrhea or constipation.

- *Inflamed redness.* This kind of redness, resulting from electrolyte imbalance, may start at the tip and then spread to encompass the whole nose. It's often called "drinker's nose" or "frosty nose" because people associate it with heavy alcohol consumption, though the common skin condition rosacea has a similar presentation. Inflamed redness may signify a sluggish metabolism and be accompanied by constant shivering, irritability, apathy, and stomach problems. When the deficiency is pronounced, the cheeks of the person with inflamed redness may take on a bluish or greenish tinge.

- *Yellow and brown discolorations* or *shadows,* caused by the same electrolyte imbalance, often accompany an inflamed red nose. They may appear at the temples, at the corners of the eyes, in front of the ears, or even all over the entire face.

- *Brownish-yellow spots* often indicate an electrolyte imbalance. These spots may be scattered across parts of the face or even all over. They may be most deeply colored along the cheekbones, and exposure to bright sun will make the spots darker. Symptoms that may accompany brownish-yellow spots include fear, grief, and anxiety. Other blotches of pigmentation on the skin, such as liver spots, age spots, and even freckles, may also indicate electrolyte deficiency.

- *Alabaster skin,* which appears milky white, is another expression of electrolyte imbalance. A slight deficiency might appear as white stripes on the eyelids and, with a more pronounced imbalance, especially in young women, the arms or other parts of the body might grow milky pale. Sometimes, the pallor will have a reddish shimmer. Other symptoms include joint problems, gout, rheumatism, inflammation, and a desire for warmth and rest.

- *Greasy skin* in an adult, especially on the forehead and sides of the nose, may signify an electrolyte deficiency. The skin may have a fatty, dull sheen, and the grease may spread to the affected person's hair and eyeglasses. Frequent washing solves the problem only temporarily. Other symptoms include heartburn, stool that's acid or fermented, and difficulty metabolizing fats.

- *Greasy stripes on the eyelids* may also reflect an electrolyte deficiency. What appears to be grease is actually more of a mucuslike substance that is sweated out through the skin. In rare cases, the substance may cover the whole eyelid or even spread down to the cheeks.

- *Blackheads and pimples* may appear in greasy-skinned people as the result of a combination of deficient electrolytes. They're actually two different things. Blackheads are clogged pores that are partly open, which turn into whiteheads if they get completely blocked. Blackheads do not appear on oily patches of skin. Pimples are blackheads or whiteheads that have become infected. The inflammation takes various forms—papules, pustules, and nodules—which can be hard to treat and may leave scars.

V. Metabolism

Face readers often see evidence that the body is not running optimally on the fuel we give it. A person may be overdoing or not effectively metabolizing one or more of the macronutrients—fats, protein, or carbohydrates—or else somehow throwing off the body's nutrient balance. As with minerals, these observations are clues to be investigated with an appropriate healthcare provider. The information in this section is not a substitute for the advice of a qualified health professional.

Fat Metabolism Disorder

There are facial signs that suggest a person is not properly metabolizing fats, putting strain on the liver and gallbladder. When face readers see the following signs, we recommend a doctor's visit for a check of cholesterol, triglycerides, and lipids, which may be at unhealthy levels. The signs include:

- Swelling under the lower lip
- Large pores in the skin at the corners of the mouth, perhaps with thickened skin and brownish-yellow coloration that,

in some cases, may extend to the whole area around the mouth, implying that liver function is affected

- Yellowish deposits at the inside part of the upper eye sockets
- A double chin and a conspicuous diagonal wrinkle across the chin (this can also be a sign of other diseases)

Protein Metabolism Disorder

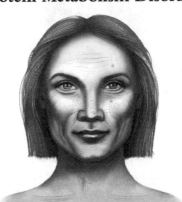

Excessive consumption of animal proteins, affecting the acidity of the body, may be reflected in the face. This is a typical disease of affluence, weakening the digestion and taxing the liver. Signs of a protein metabolism disorder include:

- Slackness of the skin below the cheekbones and, in more pronounced cases, wrinkles and fat cheeks
- Enlarged pores and a grayish cast to the skin
- If the liver is overburdened, swelling and brown shadows under the lower lip
- In women, an angular, more masculinized face ("runner's face")
- In men, loss of hair

Carbohydrate Metabolism Disorder

Excessive consumption of carbohydrates affects the blood glucose level in different ways. Simple carbohydrates, such as white flour, cause constant spikes and dips of blood sugar, while complex carbohydrates, such as whole grains, keep blood sugar levels steadier, as they are more slowly converted to energy. Those who have carbohydrate metabolism disorder are more vulnerable to the effects of blood sugar fluctuations.

The signs of carbohydrate metabolism disorder are:

- Puffiness and slackness of the skin of the lower cheeks, close to the jawline, which may develop into little pouches
- Puffiness in the area between the lower lip and bottom of the chin
- Uneven skin tone
- Areas of brownish coloration on the face, along with skin impurities, especially on the forehead

Nutrient Metabolism Disorders

The section "Minerals," above, discusses the signs of electrolyte deficiency arising either from diet or from the body's inability to absorb minerals effectively. Sometimes, however, face readers see evidence of a more general imbalance that may also involve vitamins, purines (substances in foods like organ meats, red meats, and certain seafood that raise the uric acid level in the blood and may lead to gout), pyrimidines (other important chemicals in the body), or hormones. The nature of such imbalances must be determined by a qualified health professional, and treatment may be necessary. The signs of imbalance visible in the face are:

- Skin discolorations, especially a grayish cast, and shadowy areas on the face
- Unusual shininess (or lack of shine) to the skin
- Deep wrinkles, with a swollen appearance to the skin around the wrinkles

Acknowledgments

Thank you, Jon Ellenthal, for empowering me to undertake this book. Through you, I met my brilliant literary agent Flip Brophy, who instantly grasped its potential. Flip, I'm so grateful for your faith in me, your expert guidance, and your calm, encouraging wisdom. The Sterling Lord Literistic staff—and especially the capable Nell Pierce—have sustained me with invaluable support.

Thank you, Elisa Petrini, for creating a conceptual framework for my vision and for bringing it to vibrant life. Yuliya Yarmolenka, your lively illustrations have so perfectly captured the images in my mind and memory. The two of you have expressed my work and ideas more vividly than I could have imagined.

Thank you, Joel Fotinos, publisher of the St. Martins Essentials imprint, for acquiring my book for your innovative list. You've been so warm, inspiring, and generous, easing my path though this new adventure. Gwen Hawkes, you've been a tremendous help in keeping me and the book on track.

Cristyn Girolami, your ideas and enthusiasm have always

uplifted me. A sister seeker of truth, you've opened my mind by welcoming me into your realm of like-minded knowledge hunters. Thank you for friendship, and more.

Finally, I'm indebted to those, all over the world, whose faces have been my window on human nature.

Notes

1. Our First Language

1. Jesse Gomez et al., "Microstructural Proliferation in Human Cortex Is Coupled with the Development of Face Processing," *Science,* vol. 355, issue 6320 (January 6, 2017): 68–71.

2. T. Gruter, M. Gruter, and C. C. Carbon, "Neural and Genetic Foundations of Face Recognitions and Prosopagnosia," *Journal of Neuropsychology* 2, Part 1 (March 2008): 79–97.

3. Alex Moshakis, "Super Recognisers: The People Who Never Forget a Face," *The Guardian* (UK), November 11, 2018.

4. Patrick Radden Keefe, "The Detectives Who Never Forget a Face," *The New Yorker,* August 22, 2016.

5. Steve Lohr, "Facial Recognition Is Accurate If You're a White Guy," *The New York Times,* February 9, 2018.

6. Natasha Singer, "Amazon's Facial Recognition Wrongly Identifies 28 Lawmakers, A.C.L.U Says," *The New York Times,* July 26, 2018.

7. Steve Lohr, "Facial Recognition Is Accurate If You're a White Guy."

8. Patrick Radden Keefe, "The Detectives Who Never Forget a Face."

9. Heather Murphy, "Why Stanford Researchers Tried to Create a 'Gaydar' Machine," *The New York Times*, October 9, 2017.

10. Emerging Technology from the arXiv, "Neural Network Learns to Identify Criminals by Their Faces," *MIT Technology Review,* November 22, 2016.

11. Alexander Todorov, "Can We Read a Person's Character from Facial Images?" *Scientific American* (May 24, 2018).

12. Emily J. Cogsdill et al., "Inferring Character from Faces: A Developmental Study," *Psychology Science* 25, no. 5 (May 1, 2014): 1132–39.

13. Daniel E. Re and Nicholas O. Rule, "Appearance and Physiognomy," prepublication draft from *APA Handbook of Nonverbal Communication*, ed. D. Matsumoto, H. Hwang, and M. Frank (Washington, DC: American Psychological Association, 2016).
14. Ran Hassin and Yaacov Trope, "Facing Faces: Studies on the Cognitive Aspects of Physiognomy," *Journal of Personality and Social Psychology*, 78, no. 5 (2000): 837–52.

10. Health
1. J. Chadwick and W.N. Mann (trans.), *Hippocratic Writings*, Hammondsworth, UK: Penguin (1978): 170–71.

12. Perception
1. Giacomo Rizzolatti et al., "Premotor Cortex and the Recognition of Motor Actions," *Cognitive Brain Research*, vol. 3, issue 2 (March 1996): 131–41.
2. Marco Iacoboni et al., "Grasping the Intentions of Others with One's Own Mirror Neuron System," *PLOS Biology*, 3(3): e79 (February 22, 2005).

Index